Royalties from this effort will support
The Make a Wish Foundation
for the terminally ill children of the world.

Also, proceeds will go to the
Louise Rowlett Hancock Memorial Fund
for suffering children and their families.

WAKE UP AMERICA!

Take My Heart, Take My Hand

Ann Marie Hancock

HAMPTONROADS
PUBLISHING COMPANY, INC.

Hampton Roads Publishing Company, Inc.
891 Norfolk Square
Norfolk, VA 23502
Or call: (804)459-2453
FAX: (804)455-8907

If you are unable to order this book from your local
bookseller, you may order directly from the publisher.
Call 1-800-766-8009, toll-free.

Cover design by Patrick Smith

ISBN 1-878901-68-0

10 9 8 7 6 5 4 3 2 1

Printed on acid-free paper in the United States of America

DEDICATION

I humbly dedicate this effort to Jesus Christ and His Loving Mother in the name of my precious husband of 25 years, Thomas Francis. You are the other half of my soul, "Bear." You are the living example of unconditional love. You make me better than I am.

Cori, Faith and Chip, you are the reflections of His love, and the blessings of our happy marriage.

ACKNOWLEDGEMENTS

This book belongs to the Lord and His Loving Mother as well as hundreds of their children who have contributed and supported it and me, and also to Patricio Torres. I know you are with God and His Loving Mother.

I gratefully thank Dr. Washington Winn, who delivered my beautiful children, Cori, Faith and Chip. You filled me with courage and determination, Wash. You filled me with hope during four difficult pregnancies. I love you! I thank Larry Wertz for being an inspiration to me. I am indebted to Nancy Fowler and George Collins. I couldn't have done this without you. I acknowledge Joy Guillot and Jack Sweeney. You are beautiful! I thank James Tsakanikas, who has been an incredible source of support. How could I forget Father Joachim Tierney, my "Papa," and Father Thomas Francis, my "brother." You are the wind beneath my wings. Brother DePorres, you have blessed me.

I am particularly grateful to the entire Our Loving Mother's Organization, especially Bob and Bernie Hughes, Fran McIntire, and Bernie Bourdon.

Also. . .to Rose Ann Putnam, who has prayed and fasted for me in this effort.

I thank Janie McIsaacs, Carol Bradford, Willy Kooymans, Mona Karam, Janet Amaly, Maria Bedoya, Carolyn Rithur, Kim Poole, Eleanor Ripple, Sharon Mounts, George Zajur, Jack Smith, and Juan and Louisa Ruiz.

Finally, I thank my Jewish friend and publisher, Bob Friedman, whose belief in me and patience with me has blessed me many times over, and my editor, Kathy Inman.

HIS HOLINESS, POPE URBAN VIII STATES:

"In cases which concern private revelations, it is better to believe than not to believe, for, if you believe, and it is proven true, you will be happy that you have believed, because our Holy Mother asked it. If you believe, and it should be proven false, you will receive all blessings as if it had been true, because you believed it to be true."

Pope Urban VIII, 1623-44

OBEDIENCE TO THE CHURCH

According to a decree of the Congregation for the Doctrine of the Faith, approved by Pope Paul VI on October 14, 1966, it is permitted to publish, without an imprimatur, texts relating to new revelations, apparitions, prophecies or miracles.

However, in accordance with the regulations of the Second Vatican Council, the author states that we do not wish to precede in this matter the judgment of the Church, to which we humbly submit.

Contents

Introduction   11

The Visit to Conyers   17

Interview 1 With Nancy   20

Testimony From Clergy   24

Return to Conyers   36

Simultaneous Visions of Visionaries   39

Interview 2 With Nancy   42

The Scientific Studies   50

Messages of Jesus and Mary   65

Testimony to His Love: Spiritual and Medical Miracles   85

Reflections: Diary of a Pilgrim   128

More Urgent Messages From Around the World   141

Consecrations and Prayers   183

Questions and Answers   190

Appendix 1: Correspondence From the Office
of the Archbishop of Atlanta   195

Appendix 2: The Holy Hill at Conyers   200

Introduction

Until a month ago, I thought my pilgrimages to Medjugorje, Yugoslavia, would probably be my only visits to an apparition site. I had come back to the United States with more than I had ever thought possible. I had experienced God at work. I saw the cross spin at Krizevak; I was witness to the miracle of the sun. I was privileged to go into the Room of Apparitions. I had experienced an inner peace and watched as others experienced a special healing or miracle. I would carry the memory of this oasis of peace in my heart. I would try to live the messages of peace, prayer, love, and forgiveness.

I also thought that *Be A Light* would be my final literary effort. The book has been a blessing, affording me the opportunity to meet many beautiful souls and to share in their spiritual journeys. I never dreamed I would want to write again, but here I sit, pen in hand.

Three phone calls preceded my visit to another apparition site, in Conyers, Georgia. It was the gentle urging of a friend that convinced me to pack my suitcase once again. I have great respect and admiration for Barbara Ramsey. I met her a year ago when I was lecturing in Lynchburg, Virginia. I find her to be a deeply spiritual woman as well as an extremely credible source of information. Barbara shared the story of a middle-aged wife and mother who is receiving daily visits from Jesus and his Mother Mary. The woman's name is Nancy Fowler. Barbara indicated that there had been many healings, signs and wonders in Conyers. She had been there on more than one occasion and kept a block of rooms for friends at the Holiday Inn near Nancy's home. She had a room available for my husband Tommy, our son Chip, and me.

My research on apparitions revealed something startling and exciting. Jesus and Mary are available to Nancy Fowler all day long, every day. They advise Nancy on a personal level as well as on a global level. Where else do Jesus and Mary grant such graces? This appears to be unprecedented.

The Blessed Mother has been reportedly appearing all over the world in places like Japan, Egypt, Kibeho, Africa, Ecuador, Ireland,

Syria, Yugoslavia, and now in Conyers, Georgia, USA. Since 1980 there have been a reported 300 apparition sites. Amazing!

It seems so logical to this writer that the Lord would send His Mother in times of peril. Mary represents all the compassionate, loving and nurturing qualities so sorely missed in today's world. I would also pose the question, "Who would the Lord love more than the One who with deep and compassionate love followed Him with sorrowful tears on His way to the cross?" Jesus gave us His Mother from the Cross and His love is great. Now, She gives Him back to us. Mary's messages have been consistent. She calls for prayer, fasting, and total surrender to God.

There have been many significant apparitions throughout history. Most of my readers are familiar with Our Lady of Guadalupe. The Blessed Mother appeared to Juan Diego in 1534. She identified Herself as The Mother of All Mankind. She left an image of Her face on Diego's cactus-fiber tilma. It is preserved and still displayed today.

In 1830, Our Lady appeared to St. Catherine Laboure, referring to Herself as The Mediatrix of Grace. She wept for the sons of mankind and gave the world the miraculous medal. She promised many miracles and She kept Her promise. In 1848, Mother Mary appeared to two children on a mountain top in LaSallette, France. She foretold of wars and referred to Herself as Our Lady of Tears. In 1858, she appeared to Bernadette Soubirous at Lourdes, France. She called Herself "The Immaculate Conception."

In 1917, Mary appeared to three children at Fatima, Portugal. She foretold of wars. On October 13, 1917, she promised a miracle, frequently referred to as the dance of the sun. She asked that Russia be consecrated to Her Immaculate Heart.

The current apparitions at Conyers, Georgia, bear a remarkable resemblance to those at Fatima. Our Loving Mother frequently comes dressed as Our Lady of Fatima, and She shares messages for the world on the 13th of each month. She is again foretelling wars if we do not pray and as always is asking for prayer, penance, fasting, and complete surrender to God. Mary always brings souls to the Lord. She comes as an Intercessor.

How appropriate that God chose Her, for through Her flesh and blood came the Savior of the World. Her love is deep and compassionate. Who else could have stood by with knowing and sorrowful resignation and watched while Her Son was crucified for us? Who could better teach us love and compassion than the one who exercised it every moment of Her life? How Jesus must love Her.

In 1981 the Blessed Virgin Mary appeared in the small Croatian village of Medjugorje, Yugoslavia, for the first time on the Feast of St. John The Baptist, the forerunner of Christ. On June 24, 1993, Our

Lady, Queen of Peace will have been appearing there for twelve years. She wears a crown of twelve stars. Some draw parallels to the Twelve Apostles and the Twelve Tribes of Israel and anticipate that at the conclusion of the twelve years the apparitions will cease.

There are many who believe Mary has come to the world for the final battle with Satan. She is calling us back to God. Will we listen? Jesus said at Conyers, *"Please, if you accept My love, then how can you reject My Mother? I came through My Mother and I want you, dear children, to come through My Mother on your journey back to Me."*

Infinite Love

I, the Lord, made thee.
I led thy father to thy mother.
From their union,
Of the many children that
might have been, I chose
The only person who will ever be you.

I did this knowingly.
Within you, as within all,
Lie many talents, which,
By your choosing
Can lead you to greatness
In the family of heaven.

What you might consider
to be flaws
Are particularly precious jewels.
Through their possession, and
Also by your choosing,
Great strengths of the soul can come.

Without such flaws,
Your brief years on earth
would be
A lesser testing
For you and my other children.

At this moment of birth,
With infinite love
I give to you, as to all,
My greatest gift.
I release to you life
With freedom. . .
The freedom to make what
you will
Of that which I have given thee.

Always remember, my child
I, the Lord, made thee.
I led thy father to thy mother.
From their union,
Of the many children that
might have been, I chose
The only person who will ever be you.

Anonymous

The Visit to Conyers

Tommy, Chip and I left Richmond via Delta Airlines on November 12, 1992. We were Atlanta-bound and we were not alone. The people seated behind us were discussing Conyers and how the crowds had recently grown from ten to thirty thousand pilgrims on the 13th of the month.

The Atlanta airport was busy, and the car rental area had a long line. People had come from all over America to visit a small rural area about thirty miles east of Atlanta, Georgia. The address is 2324 White Road and the name is Fowler. It is easy to find because of the red reflector lights that form a cross on Highway #138. Immediately after the turn, the statues of the Blessed Mother are obvious on the front and side properties. The statues are surrounded by flowers, and the one in the front yard is adorned with pilgrims' mementos: rosaries, pictures, petitions, etc. The statue of Our Lady of Fatima on the left side of Nancy's home was delivered December 11th, just two days before the public apparition in 1992. Many pilgrims were present that day and weekend, and many of these found a special remembrance on their photographs as the Blessed Mother herself appeared on their film. . .not an unusual phenomenon in Conyers.

Nancy's backyard is marked by a large cement cross surrounded by white plastic lawn chairs. This area is slightly raised and referred to as the Holy Hill. There will be a lengthy discussion about the Holy Hill later. Near Nancy's home is a covered area with a well and surrounding statues of forest animals and St. Francis of Assisi. Pilgrims have reported numerous healings from using the water said to be blessed by Jesus.

The property behind Nancy's home continues in a brief nature walk where one makes the Stations of The Cross. The path leads directly to a rented farmhouse, where the Blessed Mother delivers public messages on the 13th of each month. It is a pensive and quiet setting selected specifically by Jesus and His Loving Mother.

Chip, Tommy and I checked into the Holiday Inn in Conyers after 10:30 in the evening. The parking lot was full, but fortunately our room reservation was waiting for us. Morning came too soon. We were in the showers at 5:00 a.m. After a brief parking lot greeting from Barbara Ramsey and her friends, we set out for The Monastery of The Holy Spirit and 7:00 a.m. mass.

For over forty years, there has existed an order of Cistercian monks near Conyers. The spot was originally a cotton farm with a few scattered buildings. March 21, 1944, changed this because twenty Trappist monks arrived to bring Georgia a 1500-year-old tradition begun by their mentor, St. Benedict of Nursia.

After mass, our group visited The Monastery bookstore where fresh breads and jams made by the monks might be purchased in addition to desired literature. We then went over to the farm house to wait for Our Lady's visit. While usually three hours pass slowly, they did not on this day. By 9:00 a.m. the scene at the farm house was a busy one with news teams on the grounds as well as overhead in helicopters. Georgia news headlines had been captured for some time by the woman called Nancy and her Heavenly visitors. By noontime, guests numbered in the thousands. There were blankets and lawn chairs as far as the eye could see as the pilgrims recited fifteen decades of the rosary. Somewhere in the middle of the recitation, Nancy whispered that the Blessed Mother had arrived. She always comes in light and Her visits are preceded by light. How appropriate that She who is a light comes in light to remind us that we need not remain in darkness and that we are all called to the Light.

The Room of Apparitions at the farm house is not very large. The gravely sick and handicapped individuals are privileged to enter first. There is no special list of guests in Conyers. Entrance to the room is determined on a "first come, first serve" basis. I thought this served as a loving and fair reminder that we are all God's children and are equally special. It is noteworthy that there is no pushing or shoving in Conyers, but visitors move patiently and thoughtfully about.

As I looked around making some mental notes, I saw a Japanese woman holding a photo of the Mother Mary on a cloud. People were snapping cameras constantly. There was a nun carrying a religious statue that was crying bloody tears. Nancy had said the Blessed Mother had been appearing in black recently. She added that Mary mourns for those who will not return their hearts to God. She mourns for Her children. She suffers because we reject Her and She is once again giving us Her son.

I noticed many special things that day, but the greatest miracle still amazes me. It is the coming together of thousands of people in one place in love. . .people from every place and every faith. It is so moving and always reminds me of what is possible when we open our hearts to God. Sadly, I recall a statement attributed to Saul Bellow: "In experiencing love, we belong to the undeveloped countries."

(*With Love*, compiled by Evelyn L. Beilenson, Peter Pauper Press, Inc., New York, 1991.)

I had seen Nancy briefly on November 13th. I observed her spending hours talking with pilgrims after the apparition. I was deeply affected by her patience. I witnessed more of the same the following day when it was my turn to visit and ask questions.

It was 2:30 in the afternoon on November 14th that my family pulled into Nancy's driveway. There were countless pilgrims, and we could not get near the house. I could see only a little of the top of Nancy's head as she spoke from a step in her carport. We had a scheduled appointment for 3:00 p.m., but I could not see how this would materialize. For a moment I felt anxious, then a peace came over me and I grinned. If this is God's will, I would see her. I waited patiently and expectantly. At 2:50 p.m. a large group of people, tired of straining to hear, decided to leave. I stepped forward slowly and found myself directly in front of Nancy. At 3:00 p.m. she announced to her visitors that she had an appointment. Chip, Tom and I moved inside to Nancy's kitchen, where we met Ron Fowler, who stated his complete belief in his wife and in the apparitions. She had a house full of guests inside. There were priests, nuns, friends and a phone that rang constantly. My eye was drawn to a room adjacent to Nancy's kitchen. I was looking through a glass door to a beautiful statue of The Sacred Heart of Jesus. I asked if I might go in and see it. Nancy indicated that this was the Room of Apparitions in her home. As I stood close to the statue, Nancy held her face. I turned to see if I had broken the statue and I heard Nancy say, "Thank you, Jesus." I was blank as Nancy said, "Ann Marie, there is gold light pouring from your heart." She added, "I asked Jesus for a sign." I was even more confused until Nancy explained her shyness and uneasiness with reporters. I found her apparent simplicity refreshing. Her devotion to Jesus warms the heart. I could begin to understand how difficult it must be for her to suffer the rejection that visionaries must incur. I remembered Bernadette at Lourdes being arrested by French authorities in 1858. I pondered the visionaries in Medjugorje, Yugoslavia, and remembered that they had been arrested by the communists and initially rejected by friends and family. I thought about Jesus and his sufferings. It certainly was not easy for Him. Today The Blessed Mother still pleads for us to return our hearts to God. But will we listen?

Interview 1 With Nancy
November 14th, 1992, Conyers, Georgia, 4:00 p.m.

Chip and Tom set up the video recorder. I noticed that Nancy was totally unconcerned about appearance or makeup. I was reminded of how much time is spent in beauty parlors and makeup sessions. I wondered if we spend an equal amount of time on our interiors. Nancy was ready and we began with the first time she saw Jesus.

Nancy: When the visions began, I did not have a serious prayer life. I was a bench-warmer Catholic. I could not tell you what the Gospel was about five minutes after I heard it. I did not believe in visions. I was a disbeliever in demons or evil spirits. I was shown manifestations of Satan first. Boy, did it scare me to death! I was allowed to see what I did not believe existed in my own home. The Lord had to show me where I was walking. I kept seeing the kingdom I did not believe existed! It went on for months. The turning point in my life came when I went to Reconciliation (Sacrament of Forgiveness). I poured out my heart. "I'm sorry, Lord, for going the way of the world." I thought the world had all the answers. I made a sincere confession to the Lord from my heart. Then many of my fears were decreased, but not all of them. After that, though, the Lord started manifesting Himself to me in a real way. I would see light on the cross in my room in the middle of the night.

Ann Marie: Did you know ahead of time when the Lord would appear?

Nancy: I never had any knowledge ahead of time. Sometimes I was in prayer and sometimes I was not in prayer. In the beginning, I would not expect a vision.

Ann Marie: Do you remember the approximate date the Lord first appeared? Can you describe Him?

Nancy: February 1987 Our Lord appeared life-size to me in a physical glorified state. He spoke with His eyes. It was clearly the face of Jesus. I had been in a hopeless state. I was not deserving to see the Lord. He showed such love, compassion and forgiveness to me.

Ann Marie: Can you elaborate on his appearance?

Nancy: He wore a white tunic with loose-fitting sleeves.

Ann Marie: How did you feel?

Nancy: I was in a total state of awe. I felt great peace and love. I was blessed to see.

Ann Marie: Nancy, you also see the Blessed Mother Mary. When did this begin?

Nancy: The summer of 1987 I heard the voice of a lady. She said, *"My Son and I are calling you to holiness."* I said. . .My. . .that must be the Mother of Jesus. Her voice was so gentle. This was the first time I heard Her voice.

Ann Marie: If you had to sum up in capsule form the messages of Conyers, what would you say?

Nancy: If I could only use a couple of words, they would be love and mercy. We are being called back to God. Mary is the Mother to all of us; Her children need to come back.

Ann Marie: Do Jesus and Mary feel we have strayed from our hearts in this fast-paced intellectual society?

Nancy: Jesus is asking for our hearts. The heart is important to the physical body, but also to our spiritual bodies. Jesus said, *"It takes a heart to mend a heart. If someone is in pain. . .give him your heart."* Our Lady says repeatedly *"Pray from the heart."*

Ann Marie: What if you do not know how to pray from the heart?

Nancy: Our Lord takes us right where we are. Begin with one prayer from the heart. Take one step. We need to pray. Begin where you are! Not everyone can say a fifteen-decade rosary. The Lord wants us to begin to talk to Him. And Our Lady is also calling us to pray.

Ann Marie: Are these messages just for Catholics?

Nancy: Our Lady loves all Her children. This is a call to convert our hearts. Non-Catholics have been healed at Conyers.

Ann Marie: Is there an urgency in these messages? Will there be consequences for our actions?

Nancy: Yes, there is an urgency. God is a patient God. We need to focus on Him. He is a compassionate God. He is a loving God. He is also a just God. People who live in hell choose to be there. They reject God. We are loved so much that God allows us to reject Him. We make a choice.

Ann Marie: Has Our Lady spoken of consequences for rejecting God?

Nancy: Yes, She has spoken about warnings. Our Lord has given us signs. Our Lady has said there would be great waves that will hit the shores of the earth. There will be more tornadoes, hurricanes, more earthquakes. People are missing the signs and not associating them with our spiritual lives. I felt very anxious and said, "Blessed Mother, how do I fit in?" Our Lady said, *"You are just a link in the chain."* Boy. . .She put me right in my place.

Ann Marie: Has Our Lady given you a message for the Pope?

Nancy: Yes. I cannot speak of this. The Holy Father did bless my book in a general audience.

Ann Marie: Nancy, I have heard you say over and over "Love,

love, love." How though do you love the unlovable?

Nancy: I had a mystical writing experience once. I followed a light downstairs in my home. Our Lord asked me to write. I wrote nonstop and I wrote five pages. I can go get this writing if you would like me to. . .maybe it will help some people.
[Nancy left here to seek the writing.]

This was written in 1980. I will read a portion: Loving is not easy. It is not easy to love everyone. It is hard to love someone who persecutes you or accuses you falsely. It is hard to love someone when you get no love in return. How well Jesus knows about love and suffering. Loving is a growth asked of all of us. If I loved only those who loved me and said good things about me then I would remain at a pagan level and would be a dangerous witness to God. Somehow suffering and love have become one for me. As I know the reality of love, I know the reality of Jesus. It is a growth to love everyone. First, love God, then your neighbor, and our neighbor is everyone.

Ann Marie: Do you have any final words?

Nancy: I pray with all my heart that people will respond to Our Lady and God's call.

Testimony From Clergy

Father Joachim's Testimony

I left Nancy Fowler's home feeling humble and grateful for the time she shared with my family. I did ask before leaving if I might visit with her Confessor, Father Joachim Tierney. Nancy felt that would be a difficult feat to accomplish because of Father Joachim's health and busy schedule.

At 6:45 a.m. Sunday morning, November 15th, the telephone rang in our room at the Holiday Inn. Father Joachim, fondly referred to by many as "Papa," asked to see me at 8:00 a.m. at The Monastery of the Holy Spirit. Tom, Chip and I met him on time at The Retreat House. We found him to be the personification of love. His energy is boundless although he is clearly enjoying his golden years.

We sat in a small quiet room in The Retreat House adjoining the Church. Father Joachim did not mince words as he said very clearly, "I believe in Nancy. I believe in what is happening in Conyers." These are the words of the man who hears Nancy's confessions. Father Tierney did not hesitate a moment in this proclamation. We visited with him for one hour and left feeling enriched.

At 9:00 a.m., outside The Monastery, our eleven-year-old son shot some film as I did a brief commentary for writing purposes only. I closed my comments with, "Well. . .if you need a sign, maybe Conyers is the place to come." As I said this, hundreds of birds in the air as well as the Canadian geese on the ground began a loud chant and flew for a tree nearby. It was a spectacle I have never before experienced. Chip and I were stunned as were onlookers coming to The Monastery for Sunday services in the crypt. Chip and I had chills. We both had the feeling someone was speaking to our hearts. Chip and I also experienced beautiful colors, circling the sun. There was the distinct impression of a Cross formed in the sky. That Sunday at The Monastery still remains a treasured experience. The fact that Father Joachim called us remains a mystery.

Father Joachim Tierney submitted the following for this book in April of 1993. Here is his testimony in his own words.

It was in February 1989 that Nancy Fowler was introduced to me at the Monastery of The Holy Spirit. She came for the purpose of the Sacrament of Confession. From that time on I have been her confessor. At that time also, I became her spiritual director until three years hence when Archbishop Lyke of Atlanta, Georgia, asked Nancy to take a priest of the Archdiocese for her spiritual director. From the beginning of my contact with Nancy, I felt that I was dealing with a gifted soul. I was struck by her simplicity and childlike disposition. When she spoke about her conversion, of her visions of Jesus and Mary, and lights from heaven as a kind of affirmation or confirmation of what we were speaking about, I felt that I had been in some ways prepared by my own Irish Catholic upbringing, my 56 years as a monk and 48 years as a priest, to be of some help and guidance to Nancy. I believed in her from the very beginning, so much so that I have never had the slightest doubt that what she was seeing and saying was true, that what she was receiving was of Heaven and of God.

Once, in 1989, I was at Nancy's home, where she had an altar with a crucifix, pictures, statues and a lamp, which was her place of prayer when at home. Several of her friends and I were invited to pray the Holy Rosary in the prayer room. Nancy prepared a chair for me as I have a hard time kneeling without support. We had prayed several decades of the Rosary when Nancy got a message from Jesus: "Father Joachim is not comfortable." Nancy immediately tried to improve the situation.

During late Spring of 1991, Jesus appeared to Nancy and asked her to fast from all food except the Most Holy Eucharist, but she was allowed liquids. Over a month she was here at the Monastery during lunch hour, so I invited her to lunch, but she refused. Some time after that Jesus appeared and thanked Nancy for her obedience. He was satisfied with her fast. She then checked the calendar. It was exactly 40 days. During the whole period she never once felt hunger or any dizziness. She humorously made the remark, "But I still gained weight."

One afternoon, when I was returning to the Monastery after a visit to a doctor, I stopped at Nancy's home. Not wishing to bother her, I passed the house and went to the Holy Hill where I prayed two decades of the Rosary. She saw me and came out to greet me, then took me to the Apparition Room in her home, where we prayed a third decade. Our Loving Mother appeared and gave this message: "Please thank Father Joachim for doing Me the honor of visiting Me." Oh! the humility of the Holy Mother of God! Nancy remarked that this was the first time that Our Loving Mother gave a message to an individual in the room. Oh! Thank you, Loving Mother!

Nancy has been given a special gift from Jesus. She may ask Him questions and He will answer her. She hesitates to do this. Once I was with her in the back seat of one of the Monastery cars up for sale. I was thinking to myself, "Why doesn't she ask Jesus?" George Collins [who records the messages of Mary and Jesus], who was in the front seat, asked Nancy, "Why don't you ask Jesus?" I myself was interiorly pained for her not asking Jesus. Finally, Nancy did ask Him. This was the car for her. To this day Nancy is hesitant in asking things for or about herself.

The number of pilgrims visiting the Holy Hill and the Farm, where the apparitions occur on the 13th of each month, has steadily increased from hundreds to thousands. On February 13, 1993, an estimated 40,000 to 50,000 pilgrims were present, and many were turned away by the traffic policemen because of the lack of parking space. Pilgrims remain in prayer during the apparition for the three Rosaries and the message. Many times it is freezing and often raining.

Jesus has said, "By their fruits you shall know them." (Mt. 7-16) The real fruit is what takes place in the hearts, minds and souls of the pilgrims: change of heart, repentance for past sins, conversion from loss of faith to real belief in God, growth in the love of God, renewed reverence for the Most Holy Eucharist, return to devotion to the Sacred Heart of Jesus, and the Immaculate Heart of Mary. I have witnessed whole families coming back to God. Then there are also miraculous healings of the body from sickness and disease; many see the miracle of the sun. Some experience the change of silver Rosaries into gold; many are aware of the strong smell of roses, indicating the presence of the Immaculate Heart of Mary. Yes! By their fruits you shall know them!

It is a well known fact that Nancy has never once been given an interview with the Archbishop of Atlanta, or his representatives, even though Nancy has requested it a number of times. But I am happy to make this clear statement: "After over four years of contact with Nancy Fowler, as her Father Confessor, I have never had the slightest doubt that she speaks the truth, and what is happening to her is of Heaven, is of God, is of Jesus and Mary."

In the Hearts of Jesus and His Loving Mother,
Father Joachim

[Father Joachim, in this matter as in all things, acts in complete obedience to his Abbot.]

Additional Clergy Testimony

Priests and clergy have come from all over the world to Conyers, Georgia. Those I have been privileged to meet and speak with are passionate in their support of Nancy Fowler and what is taking place in Conyers. One devout priest even wrote letters to the now-deceased Archbishop Lyke. Here is the fascinating testimony of some clergy members.

I am a retired priest from the diocese of Biloxi, Mississippi. I first heard of Conyers in October 1991 from a man who just returned from there. Being a bit skeptical, I accompanied several people a week later on their visit to Conyers.

I immediately felt comfortable, as I did in Medjugorje, where I had been three times. Now I have visited Conyers on seven different occasions and have become more and more convinced of the supernatural nature of the apparitions. First of all, because of the many conversions. People who were careless or fallen away Catholics have now returned to the Sacraments and are living good religious lives.

Since I give many parish missions and retreats, I am amazed at the number of people who tell me they were away from the church and the Sacraments for years. But then they visited Conyers and their conversion began. To an individual they credit their conversion to the graces they received at Conyers.

Secondly, the apparent healings of people who attended the apparitions or prayed at the alter in Nancy's backyard or who used the healing water from the well there—people would tell me of their healings and I myself witnessed a number of them.

A physical healing was described to me by Mary Lofton of Biloxi, Mississippi. She had a nerve disorder in her right hand that kept her index finger bent down and in extreme pain. Doctors at the Biloxi Veterans' Hospital examined it and said only surgery would cure what they called in medical slang a "trigger finger." But they could not schedule surgery for several weeks. In the meantime, the pain was so intense that Mrs. Lofton could not sleep but often paced the floor in pain. One morning at 2 a.m. she remembered that someone had given her a pint jar of healing water from the Conyers well. She opened the jar and put her whole hand into the water. Immediately, the pain disappeared and as she withdrew her hand the finger was as straight as the others. The doctors at the hospital were baffled because they said this disorder could only be corrected by surgery.

In July 1992, I witnessed a lady praying at the altar in Nancy's backyard. There was an immediate change in her looks, attitude and deportment. She shared that she had attempted suicide a number of times because of depression. She decided to come to Conyers as a last resort. If she did not get some relief she would attempt suicide in a more certain way. Since then she has become a daily communicant and her life is one of peace and happiness.

Lastly, I always prayed with people in Conyers and heard their confessions. I had done this at Medjugorje and experienced the charismatic gift of word of knowledge very powerfully. Conyers was even more powerful so I knew it had to be from the Holy Spirit—only the Holy Spirit knows the secrets of a person's heart.

I always intend to remain totally loyal to our Holy Father and to the magisterium of the church. So if the church ever rules against Conyers, I will be the first to obey and not ever talk about it. But since I see so much good fruit coming from Conyers, I see no problem in telling people about it and participating in what is happening there. To me the messages are an extension of what Mary said at Fatima.

But what is most powerful about Conyers is not only Mary appearing on the 13th of each month, but that Jesus appears or speaks to Nancy almost daily. This is unheard of in most other apparitions. I know it also happened in San Nicholas, Argentina, where Jesus and Mary appeared to a native housewife during the 1980s. The church has already accepted them as authentic.

Can we be certain that what is happening in Conyers is really true? Eventually the church will make a statement. But Jesus himself gives us a clue for discerning for ourselves here and now—from Scripture. *"By their fruits you will know them."* The signs and wonders of Conyers are the best proof that Jesus and His Mother are appearing there.

I feel very comfortable with what Jesus told Nancy on December 31, 1990. *"I do not appear like this anywhere else on earth. I am giving the greatest graces here outside of My Mass. Nowhere are my graces being poured forth like they are here."*

Fr. John A. Izral

MONASTERY OF THE HOLY SPIRIT
2625 Highway 212 S.W.
Conyers, Georgia 30208

19 March 1993
To Whom it may concern:

The writer of this letter, Rev. Thomas Francis a monk and priest of the Cistercian Monastery of Our Lady of the Holy Spirit, in Conyers, GA, of the United States, can bear witness to the intense faith and piety of Mrs. Nancy Fowler. Her claim to have visions and locutions from our Blessed Lord and from Mary the Mother of God, can in my opinion, be prudently accepted as true. I have met and talked with Nancy on many occasions, and have always been impressed by her humility and willingness to submit all that she has experienced to the judgment of Holy Church, through her local bishop and clergy.

But the main source of my credence in Nancy is from the Gospel criterion: "By their fruits you shall know them." I have spoken and met with hundreds of persons who have gone to the place of the alleged apparitions. These people testify to numerous supernatural events happening there, especially of conversions, return to Sacraments and prayer; more piety, peace, love.

Sincerely in Jesus and Mary,

Fr. Thomas Francis, O.C.S.O.

MONASTERY OF THE HOLY SPIRIT
2625 Highway 212
Conyers, GA 30208

23 March 1992

Most Rev. James P. Lyke, OFM, Ph.D.
Archbishop of Atlanta

Dear Archbishop,

Permit me once again to express my gratitude that you have accepted to serve the Catholic community of North Georgia as its bishop. Your leadership over the past year has been a source of pride to us all. Just last week, I read in the Georgia Bulletin how you handled so well the volatile situation at Corpus Christi, courageously facing quite a bit of hostility. And you, with God's grace, brought it off well.

Having said and meant that, I now feel I need to express my discomfort, dismay, well, downright disappointment at the way your latest actions show you have gone from a "Gamaliel neutrality" to what I would almost call hostility to the phenomena at Conyers. Or rather, I should say to "Nancy Fowler." She was over here last evening in a very distressed condition. A priest from out of state had read to her your letter to the Bishops of USA. Today I obtained a copy of your letter (Our county newspaper already had commented on it), and so I enclose the first printed response to it. Of course I do not agree with everything Mr. Belluso writes, but there is a general empathy I feel towards his position.

To be very honest, Archbishop, I have felt all along that your refusal to talk to, or meet with Nancy Fowler is an action that I cannot justify in the light of our Jesus, who even "ate and drank with publicans and sinners." What would you think of a doctor who prescribed medicine for a patient he had never seen or examined? What would you think of a therapist who prescribed advice to a client he had never interviewed? I feel that you are in that same position. You are the representative of the meek Christ to us Catholics. Yet you refuse to meet with this person, who as you readily admit is involved "in a significant issue for the welfare of the Church in this area." You get all your information second hand, and from your well equipped office of FAX machines and copiers, you send out directives to your priests, people and now the

30

bishops of the USA. I don't see Christ Jesus working this sensitive pastoral situation in such a bureaucratic manner. I am particularly distressed because in both meeting and hearing about you, you are such a man of faith, a pastor who has admirable leadership qualities. Why then do you not meet with this person committed to your care? If you would care to share with me your reasons, it may relieve my anxiety.

Please do not for a minute think that I am trying to challenge you on your episcopal authority. You have shown admirable discretion and prudence. It is just the personal issue (as I see Jesus always meeting people, opponents or the down and out) in a humble, face to face manner. That is what I am most concerned about.

Respectfully in Jesus and Mary,

Thomas Francis

March 26, 1992

Reverend Thomas Francis
Monastery of the Holy Spirit
2625 Hwy 212
Conyers, Georgia 30208
Dear Father Francis:

Thank you for your letter of March 23, 1992, regarding the situation in Conyers.

Father, I recognize that from your prospective I appear rather uncaring and unsolicitous about Nancy Fowler and the people who come to Conyers.

In response, let me say that, having observed the situation there, spoken with Father John Walsh, and having met with the civic authorities, I have acted in the way that I see most suitable to this issue. The letter which I addressed to the bishops of the United States is based upon the fact that the Church does not want its bishops to give affirmation to alleged apparitions in any way. As you know, the Church has traditionally been extremely cautious regarding such alleged apparitions. When I recently spoke with the Pro Nuncio he was satisfied with the way I am handling the situation.

I do not doubt Nancy Fowler's sincerity or faith. The alleged apparitions are not, in the end, about Nancy Fowler. They are about whether, in fact, apparitions have taken place. Thus far, I have no evidence of this. When evidence occurs, I will be happy to examine this situation again.

You must realize that 99% of these so called apparitions have not been authenticated by the Church, and they have passed away with time. It is for such reasons that the Church has always been extremely cautious. I intend to maintain such caution here in the Archdiocese of Atlanta.

I have made provisions for Father John Walsh and the people of St. Pius X Church to respond to the pastoral needs of the people. He and his staff and parish are doing a fine job of that. These pastoral needs do not need to be taken care of at the Monastery or at the site of the alleged apparitions.

I respect the fact that you disagree with me. However,

32

having reflected often enough on this matter, I continue to affirm and implement the directives that I have given.

May the Lord bless and keep you.

In the Peace of Christ,

> Most Reverend James P. Lyke, O.F.M., Ph.D.
> Archbishop of Atlanta

cc: Abbot Dom Bernard Johnson, O.C.S.O.
Father John Walsh

[2nd Letter]
Holy Spirit Monastery
2625 Highway 212
Conyers, Georgia 30208

March 31, 1992

Most Rev. James P. Lyke, OFM, Ph.D.
Archbishop of Atlanta

Dear Archbishop,

Your long, personal letter, was indeed a surprise to me, and I wish to express my gratitude for your taking the time to express-explain your approach to the "situation" in Conyers. I liked your last paragraph where you mention you respect the fact I disagree with you, and once again you affirm satisfaction with the way you address the issues.

OK. OK. I realize you are not open to dialogue on your present procedures, and I respect your decision. BUT, let me express my disappointment that you chose, in response to my letter, to ignore the central and burning issue I brought up: namely, the DANGEROUS MEMORY of Jesus. Who always chose to meet and dialogue with people, be they enemies, strangers, ignorant or whoever. (Let me further recall that your patron, St. Francis, acted in the same way, even preferring the lowly and the ignorant! Remember how he adamantly refused to cave in to the demands of Cardinal Ugolino and Pope Innocent III as regards poverty. Then too his humble but personal appearance to the mighty Sultan of Egypt. Oh, for some Franciscan bishops of that stature!)

I might also remind you that not only myself, but others who know you refuse to meet with Nancy Fowler (because she complains to them of your lack of personal contact with her), have serious problems with your credibility. I must admit that I have lost esteem for your pastoral judgment, as you continue to act on 2nd hand information in so important a matter. Yet, I promise to obey you and your directives, and exhort others to do so as well. You are our bishop, not Nancy or anyone else. With Francis, both your and my patron, obedience to the bishop and the Pope are unquestionably the signs of loyalty to Jesus and His Kingdom.

Now for a piece of good news: Sunday evening Nancy

34

phoned me that she could not come to the Gospel lesson. She then asked me what I thought of the suggestion a priest made to her of going to the Franciscan University of Steubenville to get "checked out" by a psychiatrist there. I immediately told her I thought it was a great idea and that she should act on it as soon as she reasonably could. I mentioned that both the civil and ecclesiastical authorities would be influenced in their decisions, if they had competent medical testimony as to her Mental-psychological health. (Archbishop, perhaps you might say that I too need to be "checked out!")

In Jesus and Mary, whom we both love and serve,

Fr. Thomas Francis, OCSO

[No response was received to this letter.]

Return to Conyers

I know now that it was no coincidence that I returned to Conyers for The Feast of The Immaculate Conception, December 8th, 1992. The night before my departure from Richmond I developed a sore throat. By the morning of December 7th I had lost my voice. Many who know me would say it was a blessing and they were right. I was speechless December 8th, and yet I was poised with my tape recorder to do more interviews with Nancy for this book. I must have been an amazing sight.

When I walked back into Nancy's bedroom that morning I found her with tissues in the bed. She had the flu and was losing her voice. Nancy was distressed that she was too ill to attend mass on Mary's Special Feast Day. We sat on her bed sucking on cough drops.

Nancy's phone rang constantly that day. She spent time with each person who called her. I remembered a man who had come to see her a month earlier. It was cold that day, and Nancy had spent forty minutes with him as if he were a long lost brother.

My mind drifted back to the present moment, when a blue-eyed blonde woman named Carol Bradford entered the room. I squeaked out my name, and, after a friendly exchange, Carol asked me to join her for mass at The Monastery of The Holy Spirit. I love The Monastery and the feeling I have when I visit there. I also knew I might get to visit with my friend, Father Joachim. . ."Papa."

The mass was particularly special this day. People consecrating their hearts to the Immaculate Heart of Mary were being recognized. I wore my Kleenex out as a family of five consecrated their hearts to The Blessed Mother. My heart ached to be part of the ceremony and anointing, but I was not prepared.

Feeling a little sad, and still suffering from laryngitis, I decided to visit with the beloved "Papa," who would fix everything. Father Joachim had many visitors that morning, and we had to wait for him. I decided to go outside. I should be embarrassed to tell you what happened next, but I feel in my heart that I must. I asked that perky blue-eyed blonde if she would walk down in the parking lot with me while I smoked a cigarette. Smoking is a habit of mine I am less proud of than others. Carol Bradford blurted out "No you're not. . .you've had your last cigarette." I could have crawled under the sidewalk and I wouldn't have made a lump.

While in a state of shock, I persisted, "I just want one."

Carol looked at me and said, "If you smoke I will get down on my knees in the parking lot and pray for you." I was horrified! She said, "Addictions do not belong to Christ and you belong to Him." Now, I had laryngitis and a bad case of nausea. To appease Carol, I did not smoke. I still was not sure about what she had said to me. I did however think about my family and the clouds of smoke I had created for years in our family room at home. I suddenly felt a little selfish. My family never criticized me, but they did ask me repeatedly to quit for my own sake because they loved me. My nausea was getting worse!

The Monastery bookstore offered a temporary refuge and escape from my thoughts and the awkwardness of the moment. Then, Carol appeared again and said she had purchased a gift for me. She presented me with a prayer book of St. Bridget of Sweden. She said she felt that I was supposed to have it. Carol Bradford knew nothing about me. We had never met before December 8th in Conyers, Georgia. It is significant that you know I graduated from St. Bridget's School in Richmond and I attend St. Bridget's Church. I felt a lump in my throat as I flipped my gift over, and on the back was St. Gertrude. I graduated from St. Gertrude's High School as President of the Student Body in 1964. I could not look at Carol. The tears just came as though someone had opened a floodgate. I felt relief, peace, and a fear of failing Christ and myself. Carol said, "You won't fail." She was so sure. She said, "It's the end, it's over." She added that she had never approached anyone like that before, but that she was totally guided to do so. I was particularly moved when Carol told me she was Lutheran. She had asked me to take her guardian angel with me to Communion that morning.

I will never forget that morning. God sent an angel to me. For the first time in a long time I feel free. I love you, Carol.

The day was to bring even more joy and surprises. We returned to Nancy Fowler's home and brought her lunch. Nancy was gracious, but not hungry. She wanted us to go out in the yard and greet pilgrims. Janie McIsaac had now joined us. She is a lovely woman and without a doubt Nancy's right arm. The three of us went out back to the Holy Hill and were joined by another friend Willy Kooyman, and two strangers. One of the strangers in the husband/wife duo was blind.

The group of six began to pray. It was about 4:00 in the afternoon, and it was cold and overcast. In the words of Carol Bradford, my new Lutheran friend, I submit, unedited, her account of what happened.

The six of us started to pray and we noticed the sun spinning, dancing and getting brighter. The area around the sun became blue, pink, green, yellow and then we became bathed in gold light. Even the blind man was able to see the colors, and he commented on the beauty. I turned to him and said, "Didn't you say you were blind?" He said, "I am, but I can see the colors." At this time, Ann Marie Hancock was holding a relic containing a piece of the cross of Jesus Christ. The cross began to bleed. It looked as though there was blood on Christ's arms and legs. We could all see this. As we continued to pray we saw a heart form in the sky. Gosh, what a miracle for God to give such a heavenly display for just a few of us. We all felt blessed and privileged to experience this. Ann Marie took a picture and The Blessed Mother came out on the film.

Signs and wonders of God's love abound in Conyers. There is no doubt that we are all called to the light but will we respond?

Simultaneous Visions of Visionaries

I had a conversation with a respected clergyman just previous to the publication of this book. I had told that priest that Nancy had visions together with a visionary in the United States and one in Venezuela. The priest commented that to his knowledge this was unprecedented in this history of apparitions. He asked me if I was sure of this. Here now is the testimony of Carol Ameché of Scottsdale, Arizona.

April 20, 1993

Dear Ann Marie,

On a Saturday afternoon in February, Gianna Talone, the purported visionary from St. Maria Goretti Church in Scottsdale, Arizona, where my husband and I attend Mass and prayer groups, came over to our home at our invitation to pray a Rosary with our guests, Anne and Joe Weibel from Vero Beach, Fla., "Mary and Terry" from another part of Fla., Fr. Tim from Sebastian, Fla., and Nancy Fowler with her "scribe," George Collins from Conyers, Ga.

I had invited Gianna to pray and meet with Nancy in order to make her feel as welcome as possible and to acquaint the two "alleged visionaries." It was rather late in the day, so Gianna suggested a Chaplet of Divine Mercy after we had looked at some of the pictures taken in Conyers at Nancy's place of apparition. We all prayed slowly and quietly around the coffee table and in front of corner shelves on which stood a beautiful statue (brought to us by Nancy) of Our Loving Mother, the title given by the Blessed Mother when She reportedly appears in Conyers. At the end of the chaplet, Gianna suddenly looked up and said to all, "Can we please kneel?" She quickly came over to kneel next to me and whispered, "Our Lady is coming," in a very surprised voice.

We knelt down immediately and watched Gianna and

Nancy focus totally on the statue of Our Lady, Gianna's face rather animated and her head nodding occasionally; Nancy's face more quiet and reserved, but smiling faintly.

After several minutes, both young women lowered their heads for a few moments. Then Gianna moved over to where Nancy had remained seated, and they began an animated conversation. Since they made no attempt to hide their excitement or words, we could hear them saying, Gianna: "She gave you to me as a sister and told me to pray and support you;" Nancy: "She told me She was giving us to each other as sisters, and that you would be praying for me and supporting me!!!" Both girls definitely had light shining from their faces and were bubbling over with delight. Gianna related that she was very surprised Our Lady had come to her so early in the day, since She always appears to her on Saturday evening at her own home during a recitation of the Rosary. My husband and I have been present at her home on several occasions when this occurred. Nancy was just plain overjoyed that Blessed Mother had spiritually "joined" the two of them; and it came to me she must be filled with gratitude since I had heard that much of Nancy's time spent in Conyers dealing with alleged apparitions of Our Lady had been a time of personal struggle, ridicule and rejection.

We were all filled with wonder and awe that Our Lady should have come to our home; graced all of us in such a way; gifted the two women in this very special way; and confirmed Her presence by giving both the same message.

The previous night, Nancy had related to us during a Rosary that the statue she had brought to us, which we had put on top of an armoire for want of a better place, had continually moved over to the top of the corner shelving and back again. It is Nancy's "style" to report aloud what she is seeing during an apparition or vision, and we were all amazed! Light had surrounded Her there, Nancy said, and she later told us that many blessings would come to people who came to our home and prayed, and that the light around the statue would become more visible to all, as time went by. We have since moved and hope the light and special gifts have followed Her to a new corner of our new home!!!

We had been filled with delight to meet Nancy; get to know her wonderful sense of humor and sincere humility, but added to that was a new sense of excitement at the gifts given to all who gathered to once again honor Our Blessed Mother with love and prayers.

I don't see the "light" yet, myself, but my husband has on several occasions (sigh. . .drat. . .wouldn't you know it. . .men!) We are getting settled quickly and look forward to many people praying here; and the return of George and Nancy and the wonderful graces and stories about Jesus and Mary which seem to accompany them everywhere they travel. We certainly thank God for sending them to our house!!

Interview 2 With Nancy
December 11, 1992

The day before I was to leave Conyers for home, Nancy and I were both feeling better, and our voices had partially returned. The events of December 8th served to remind me, however, that sometimes words are not necessary. I was reminded of the statement, "Be still and know that I am God."

On December 11th, Nancy granted a two-hour interview, the transcription of which follows.

Ann Marie: Nancy, there are so many who don't know how to begin their spiritual lives. Some are even afraid. What do you say to them?

Nancy: The Lord knows us completely. He loves us completely and unconditionally. We should begin simply to speak to Him honestly and from our hearts. Say "Lord take me now and mold me. . .change me." There is no formula for prayer. It is simply talking to God from our hearts. God loves us right here and right now where we are.

Anne Marie: What about those who feel lost?

Nancy: That the Lord would appear to me should serve as a lesson. I was not deserving to see God. . .wretched sinner that I am. God is so great! He is a God of unconditional love and forgiveness and mercy. All human love, even the best of relationships, is just a mere reflection of God's love. We have so many conditions to our love. God has none. If we would just go to Him.

Ann Marie: You have not always lived here in Conyers. I understand there is an interesting story, Nancy. Would you share it?

42

Nancy: Jesus spoke to me one day. I was granted a vision. I was living in a small apartment in Norcross. My husband had been sent overseas on business for the government. He was employed in the Civil Service.

You know Jesus appears to me over the Crucifix. I see the glorified risen Christ. He appears to me daily. The Lord told me I was moving. Then I saw a large cross made of stone on a hill. I saw a statue of The Blessed Mother at the foot of the cross. There was a statue of The Sacred Heart of Jesus in the middle of the cross. I saw The Blessed Mother in the sky. Then the vision was taken from me. I knew I had to find this house. My friend George Collins called. I told him about the vision. He asked if I wanted help. George has some experience with real estate. George knew where a lower-income family would live. I'd been to Conyers once to visit The Monastery of the Holy Spirit. I thought perhaps the land would be around a tabernacle. It seemed a logical place. We looked around the Pius X church. . .we found the house in three hours' time. I guess I looked like a pretty unusual person. People would tell us about the house amenities, and I'd run to the back window looking for a hill. The real estate man said, "Don't you like any of them?" I said, "Oh yes, they're all fine, but I'm looking for a special backyard." He said, "Oh, I have lots." As we drove on, George turned right on a dust road. I said, "No. . .turn left. . .and there was a tiny sign "for sale by owner." I heard the words "This is it." I didn't tell George because he has so much faith, he wouldn't show me any more houses. I ran to the back and there was a hill. The next day, I went to see the inside of the house. "Oh boy, the inside was rough; everything was broken. In one of the children's rooms there was a big hole and you could see right through to the basement.

I went home to pray. That night Jesus appeared to me, and He knew I wasn't happy with the house. I said, "Jesus, is this what you want me to buy?"

Ann Marie: Nancy, I don't mean to interrupt, but it is so hard for me to understand that you would question what Jesus asked of you. Do you always address Him that personally?

Nancy: Oh my—yes! Jesus is very alive. He is with us everywhere. We just don't consciously believe it. Jesus always shows me what I need. He is my best friend. He is your best friend. He wants an intimate relationship with us.

Ann Marie: Let's talk some more about this. I love your expression that "Jesus is alive and with us." Certainly, I believe this; however, I think many think of Him up and out there somewhere and address Him more formally. Who are we kidding? He knows us completely, our thoughts and how we express ourselves. He sees us everywhere and every way. I suppose we could wear all kinds of faces and costumes, but He knows! Why do you think we struggle with the right words?

Nancy: We put God in a box. We think He can't do this or wouldn't do that. He is God! He can do anything! He is a spouse—your best friend—your Father—your brother. He is so alive! If we knew Jesus, we'd want to help everyone. There would be no jealousy, only happiness. We would want to be just like Him. He is everything. You should be able to go to Him. He wants us close to Him. We are in the palm of His hand. You know, Ann Marie. . .God has a sense of humor, too.

Ann Marie: I find it difficult to believe that God never laughed or enjoyed laughter. So often I think about the laughter of little children. . .How contagious and joyful it is.

Nancy: Just this week I was being stubborn about some things and I wouldn't concede to some fine plans my husband was trying to make for the holidays. Jesus said, *"You are a very difficult child, Nancy; I love you very much."* I looked at Jesus and said, "You must hate me." Jesus said, *"How could I ever hate you? You are part of me. I love you, and I am Perfect Love."*

Ann Marie: Nancy, I have two questions. What advice would you share to help people begin to understand the depth of God's love? Certainly the total depth is beyond our comprehension. How can we remember His love more consistently than we do?

Nancy: I love what God said to me about love. He said, *"Take the L—Love is Life. Life is love. Take the O—the circle of love and put it around yourself and extend it to your family, friends, community. Make the O circle bigger. Make the circle grow. Then you become closer to Me. The larger circle of love gets, the closer you get to Me. Take the V—you'll be victorious over Satan. Take the E—then you have eternal life. Love is light."* Our journey on earth should be a journey of love.

Ann Marie: As you have become closer to God, have you found yourself waking up, looking in a mirror and seeing a new person?

Nancy: The closer you get to God, love becomes a given. You start to think of others, not yourself. You become more loving, more giving. We need to remember—we are always affecting another's soul.

Ann Marie: What keeps us from loving?

Nancy: We forget to focus on the Lord. We need to focus. We need to keep our eyes on the Lord. Only then will we see Christ in every person. Our Lady said, *"Be loving; be giving. Do nothing to lose a soul. There is nothing more important than a soul. Never use unkind words."*

Ann Marie: What do you say to the atheist, Nancy?

Nancy: I begin by dying to myself. Do not think of self. We have only to love, because God is perfect love. I say look around you; look at nature; look at the sky; look at the earth. See the buds and others around you. Notice the little flowers. See a blade of grass. Wouldn't the atheist say, "I don't believe in God?". . .a blade of Grass? I would say, see God in a blade of grass. God gave me a teaching one day. God knows the blade of grass and which way it will move before it even moves. He knows when it will be cut and even if it will die of thirst. God said, *"Consider the fields of grass in the world."* The Lord knows how many—do you? Now. . .he loves us! Each of us! No matter what gifts we have they are from God and are to be used to help each other. Remember you can't tell me about those blades of grass, but God can—only God!

Ann Marie: What would be the perfect prayer?

Nancy: One day I was overcome with love and spirit. I asked the Lord for the best prayer. The Lord said, *"One from the heart."* I suggest, keep it simple: for instance, "Good morning, Lord. Good morning, Mother Mary. I love you."

Ann Marie: Is the Lord distressed when we are distracted?

Nancy: The Lord takes us right where we are. Be honest. God alone is perfection. God loves us in spite of ourselves. Begin with honesty because God knows everything. Say, "Lord, there is a ball game today; I'd really like to see it, but I'm here Lord; I'm trying; Lord, I don't know what to say." The Lord honors our honesty. He knows our every thought, so be honest. He loves that we try. If the mind wonders, it's okay. God knows our imperfections.

Ann Marie: What about those in a state of total despair?

Nancy: It's never too late for anyone. God's love and mercy is endless. The greatest tragedy is to give up and despair of God's love and mercy. Just call the Lord. Just say his name. I was at the lowest point when Jesus came to me to remind me of his love and mercy.

Ann Marie: Parents seem to be struggling today with their children. Does Our Lord address this?

Nancy: Yes! He says, *"If you want holy children, be holy* *parents. "* The Lord wants prayer back in the homes. Our strength comes from God. We need Him in our families. We need Him in our homes.

Ann Marie: Our Lady appears in black often now. Why?

Nancy: She cries for her children. Mary wants us to trust and know God. She wants us to imitate Christ. She wants us to stop offending God. She wants us to love and forgive. She wants to see love and patience in all things. Ann Marie, we've stopped praying in America.

Ann Marie: Does Our Lord give you teachings on patience?

Nancy: Yes. The Lord is with us all the time. He wants to help us. One winter morning, my son James was about five years old and he had these pajamas with a zipper. James took them off four times and I put them on four times; and the fifth time he came in dangling them on his fingers—Jesus was appearing to me at that moment. I cried, "Okay James, not again!" I asked the Lord to help me.

Ann Marie: [laughs] You actually asked Jesus to do something with James as we might ask our husbands for help in the same situation. What happened?

Nancy: I was ashamed. I thought Christ would take my side and say, "Be a good boy, James," but he didn't. Christ said, *"If James takes them off five times, put them back on five times in love and patience. "*

Ann Marie: I am grinning, Nancy, only because most of us would have said, "I'm sorry, Lord. . .he doesn't act like this all the time." Do I really think the Lord can't see and that he doesn't know how my son acts? It's funny how we fool ourselves.

Nancy: The Blessed Mother says by being humble, we affect more positive changes. Everything must be done in honesty, love and patience.

47

Ann Marie: Changing the subject, what should people coming to Conyers expect? Or should there be expectations? Should people expect healings?

Nancy: We should pray for God's Holy Will. We should put everything in His hands. We should ask that God's Will be done. God answers all prayers. We must trust God. God doesn't miss a single prayer.

Ann Marie: Nancy, I love to think about our Lord's sense of humor. I would think it would be helpful in dealing with all His children. Would you share a final example with us?

Nancy: I have a memory of purchasing a face cleaner in a discount store. I went into the bathroom to apply it and the cleanser turned blue on my face. I crossed in front of the Cross to find a face cloth. I heard Jesus say "You look funny." Jesus was smiling. I was looking at Him with a blue face. I wanted to cry in that moment. I was so touched that He had time to tease me. I thought "Oh Lord, you always have time for me. Your love is so great. You are always with us."

God is alive! He loves us. We should desire a warm relationship with Him. We should have a warm relationship with God. He is so patient, so good, so warm, so loving, so forgiving.

Ann Marie: Nancy, does the Lord ever reprimand you?

Nancy: Oh my, yes! I am so deserving of severe words, but He does everything in love and patience and never in anger. I can only speak of Him as Love and Mercy. He is so great!

Ann Marie: Does the Lord express disappointment in us as parents?

Nancy: His love is endless, but a good parent reprimands his child if he cares about him; Jesus always corrects in love. I cry during apparitions. I cry tears of joy for His love is so perfect.

Ann Marie: I'm confident, Nancy, that there will be those who will have difficulty with this story about the face cream. *But maybe this incident calls for us to examine our relationships with God.* Christ is calling us to an intimate relationship with Him. His love is so great. He doesn't want to be left at the church service on Saturday or Sunday. It would seem He is reminding us in warm, special ways that He is alive and with us. Thank you, Nancy.

The Scientific Studies

The author finds Dr. Philip Serna Callahan's testimony, which follows, to be remarkable. I had a conversation with Dr. Callahan one month before publication of this book. The scientist is internationally recognized for his studies involving extensive artistic and infrared analysis of the Image of The Virgin Mary in the basilica of Guadalupe. He also worked with the scientific team performing studies on the Shroud of Turin. Dr. Callahan appeared on NBC's "Unsolved Mysteries" during Easter week of 1993. He expressed total belief in Nancy Fowler.

Dr. Ricardo Castañón spoke with me from Bolivia in April of 1993. He remains convinced of Nancy Fowler's authenticity as a messenger from God.

Here are the scientific studies of the experts. Their reports are reproduced, unedited, as they were presented. You decide!

Study 1

On May 14, 1992 my wife Winnie and I were travelling home from Pennsylvania to Gainesville, Florida when we decided to stop in Conyers, Georgia where we had heard of a series of apparations occuring to a Nancy Fowler.

We found her talking to a group in front of her home. There was also an Australian T.V. crew filiming the event and the visionary.

We introduced ourselves and I told her about my scientific work on the Image of Our Lady of Guadalupe and the Shroud of Turin.

Nancy Fowler was most garcious and told us she would be more than delighted to work with us while she was in the meditative state on the 13th of June. We could not be with her on that particular date as we had plans to be in Ireland but could be with her on July 13th. 1992. Nancy did not in any attempt to discourage us, but seemed most eager to have me present during the apparation.

We returned early July 13th. 1992 at 8:00 AM.

I spent the morning up to 10:30 measuring the Atmospheric Schumann frequencies on the cross hill near the apparation room. The ELF Schumann atmospheric frequencies, 1 to 70 Hz, were extremely high in the area. This is generally true of all apparation sites I have measured eg. Knock, Kerrytown Ireland, Lourdes, and La Salette, France and Medugorji. The VLF atmospheric frequencies from 100 Hz to 400 KHz were also very strong as is usual in apparation areas.

We entered the apparation room at 11:00 AM with Tom Harris, to record my readings, and Winnie, my wife to photograph the proceedings, (nothing of importance appeared on the photographs).

Nancy Fowler agreed to hold my recently invented PICRAM (Photonic Ionic Cloth Radio Amplifier Maser, recently patented) between her folded

2

hands for the entire period.

Astonishly the oscilloscope showed that within 20 to 30 seconds Nancy went into the 8 Hz meditative state. The human body acts as an antenna-amplifier for the Schumann waves (1 to 70 Hz) just as it does in the broadcast radio region eg. touch a reciever antenna and the sound increases. Everyone I ever measured resonates between 14 and 28 Hz while awake, not at 8 Hz as. if in the alpha meditative state and alpha atmospheric state.

Even more astonishly she soon started generating what are known as group or bullseye waves (waves that go out in ripples from the center like throwing a rock in water).
It would take a text book of mathematics to explain the physics of such waves. I have never received such energy from any living creature before (plants or animals) with my detector and oscilloscope.

While measuring Nancy at about 12:45 PM there were three bright flashes of light in the room. Nancy had announced this is the sign Our Blessed Mother is leaving the room (no camera flashes were allowed) Quite a few people also saw the three flashes.

My wife , Winnie also observed a halo around the statue, I did not.

At about 12:30 PM my scope battery warning (5mins left on battery) went on. The scope continued to operate three hours after the battery should have been discharged - I have no explaination for this phenomenon except that all of my messages at such places, eg. Laser lines (light) from the church steeple in Medgugorji have been electronic and technical - scientific one might say!

There is no question in my mind that Nancy Fowler is a true visionary

3

This is in the nature of a very short report as I have five pages of notes that my wife and I wrote up after our scientific and spiritual experience while driving home.

It is indeed sad that many people (church and otherwise) seem to believe that Americans are not allowed by God to have visionaries - only people who live in far off exotic places!

2016 N. W. 27th. Street
Gainesville, Fl. 32605
11-2-1992

Dear Nancy:

First let me thank you for your many kindness to Winnie and me on the thee occasions we visited you.

I am delighted with the research we began with you - I feel the Virgin Mary is directing it.

Tom Harris called and said you would like to know more about what I am detecting with my instrument.

In terms of the enviornment I am measuring a frequency or frequencies in the atmosphere generated by lightning around the world.

Flashes of lightning anywhere in the world "light" up the atmosphere with radio waves the same way electricity "lights" up the gas in a fluorescent tube. They are called Schumann waves.

The only difference is that instead of the light being visible (in the visible spectrum) it is invisible in the radio spectrum of long waves. The waves range from 1 cycle per second (1 Hertz) to 80 Hertz. Hz is the symbol for cycles per second.

Normal waves in most places are from 14 to 25 Hz in the air. Where the Virgin appears they vary from 6 to 10 Hz.

Our brain waves give off 8 Hz when a person (eg. Saint) is in the meditative state. Usually I measure 14 Hz to 18 Hz for most people all day long.

When you Kneel or stand before a beautiful statue of Mary and have your visions your waves drop from 14 to 16 down to 6 to 10 -- even more remarkable they vary from 6 to 10 in a wave configuration called soliton waves, that is waves on waves and in groups of waves called target or bullseye waves because they go out at varying frequencies like waves from a pebble thrown in a puddle of water.

TOP VIEW   ROCK
CLOSER & CLOSER

ON MY OSCILLOSCOPE — SIDE VIEW

Such group waves ride piggy back on regular sine waves.

GROUP WAVE
SINE (PHASE) WAVE
REGULAR

2

A regular sine wave is called a phase wave.

Since a sine phase wave is like a steady tone, it can not carry a message but a group wave can because it come along like dots(·) and (-) dashes.

Complex math called Maxwells wave equasions predict, of necessity (we design radio and TV antenna with Maxwells equasions) that phase wave travels faster than the speed of light whereas group waves travel slower than the speed of light. The speed of light is 300,000,000 meters per second equal to 186,000 miles per second.

We may understand then that your waves between 6 to 10 Hz cover the meditative alpha state or, as psychologists say the altered state, and contain an information component group (bullseye) waves (𝓥𝓥𝓥) and faster than light component phase wave (∿∿). A message carried by phase waves (carrying piggy back group waves) could arrive by photons in the past; or future (faster than light).

I have obtained such phase and group waves (solitons is the $10 physicist name) in only two other places. One, the top of a 150 foot, 12 feet in diameter (enclosed picture) kapok tree deep in the Amazon jungle. It was obtained by sending a very gentle Indian climber up the tree with my oscilloscope detector,

Two, I have obtained them, and do so every day at dawn and dusk, in a special chamber called a Reich Box. The Reich box is known for certain to heal people despite the evil ways of the AMA. I hope you will pardon my disgresson but I do believe that modern medicine is driven by greed, as is chemical agriculture!

In areas of the world where Mary has appeared phase waves (faster than light) occur in the 8 to 14 Hz region and 5 to 10 times stronger than elsewhere. This included Conyers, Lourdes, Medugorji, Knock, Kerrytown and LaSalette, all of which Winnie and I have visited.

We may further understand then that in places where gentle visionaries see .Mary both "message waves" and "faster than light waves" of the atmosphere match (resonate too) the altered state (meditative wave) of visionaries. It is God's way of doing things (miracles) by utalizing what He created, that is nature. Real scientists study and work with nature and do not destroy it as does modern high energy technology.

With that statement I feel I should define my concept of miracles. This is so because one of the questions most asked of me is why do I want to investigate Mary'y appearances on earth. The question implies that if I really believed I would not need science to prove it. The answer is, of course, quite simple, If Christ did not wish to send us signs to meditate upon He would not have bothered healing, or even, for that matter rising from the dead. Science is the detailed study of nature and since God manipulates nature to perform miracles, then the study of miracles is a form of

3

meditation on God's wonders.

Itwas St. Augustine himself who said in the "City of God" that miracles are temporal, "of this world". The word supernatural has been distorted by modern theologians to mean beyond nature, whereas what it really means is, that God uses what He built (nature) to send His messages to mankind and to reassure, in mans mind, His everlasting presence.

It is sad that it often seems to the public that scientists compete with one another for great prizes and recognition, which is not of itself bad, but does more often than not obscure what science is really all about - a recognition of God's great love of mankind by providing man with the wonders of nature, and also providing the scientist with the mind and curiosity to study His great masterpiece.

As you may understand Nancy it should not be considered unusual that these days Mary is sent quite often from God as his messenger, for today mass technological war against nature and also war against a true moral love of God threatens all of us.

God Bless and lots of LOVE.

Phil & Winnie Callahan.

Study 2

"INTERNATIONAL CENTER FOR HUMAN STUDIES

"GROUP FOR PEACE"

NANCY FOWLER'S VISIT TO

BOLIVIA

February 28 - March 8

La Paz - Bolivia

1993

"INTERNATIONAL CENTER FOR HUMAN STUDIES"
"GROUP FOR PEACE"

P.O.Box, SM: 12366   Tel. 02-79 52 64 - 79 58 00
La Paz - Bolivia   Fax: 591-2- 35 47 46

NANCY FOWLER'S VISIT TO BOLIVIA
FEBRUARY 28 - MARCH 8 1993

I. BACKGROUND:

A 43 years old university professor, graduated in clinical psychology, with specialty in psychosomatic medicine and neuropsychophysiology has been away from religion for about 22 years and on June 5, 1992, he arrives home at 19.00 and smells a fragance. He thinks it is the office deodorant, but the next day, on June 6, he again feels the same perfume, he thinks it is like violet perfume, an the other person who is with him smells it too.

In the company of the person mentioned above, he feels the need to look for a book that was lent to him a month earlier and which did not interest him at all. At night, he gets up, looks for the book, begins to read it and remembers the title: "THE QUEEN OF THE COSMOS". It is about the Medjugorje Virgen apparitions. He reads half of the book, goes to sleep. He awakes the next day and reads it again. At noon, he feels the need to pray, but he does not remember any prayer. He looks for a Bible at home, but he does not find any. He goes to his mother's home, tells her about his urge to pray. His mother knows he has been away from religion, an atheist, etc., she surprises, understands and says:"¡Son, today is June 7, Holy Spirit's Day, it is Pentecost, you are converting!".

Baffled, this gentleman gets more interested in Medjugorje, begins to pray, reds several books that a priest lends to him. He wirtes 3 pamphlets explaining the facts about Medjugorje and he finds out through a vide that the Virgen also appears to a lady by the name Nancy Fowler in Conyers, Atlanta.

On September 1st., 1992, he travels to Conyers to be present during the September 13 apparitions, since he finds out that the Virgen Mary appears every thirteenth of each month to give a message to the U.S.A.. His mother gives him as a present a white rosary with silver chains. After a few days in Georgia, in order to orientate a programed stay of two weeks, he arrive to Conyers.

On September 4th, he arrives at Conyers, stays in the Villager Lodge, at 16.00 he goes in a taxi to visit the "Holy Hill", goes to the place where the apparitions take place and after two hours he returns to the Hotel. The place is quiet, the evening is still clear, he decides to take a walk, carries the rosary with him to pray during the walk and he notices that the links of the chain of his ROSARY HAVE TURNED GOLDEN. Surprised, he does not believe, he thinks that they were always golden, and he feels a great numbness. The next day, he visits the "Holy spirit Convent" and a Lady whom he did not know, shows him a rosary saying that hers has turned golden. The bolivian pilgrim notices that it is of the same golden color that his rosary turned into.

In the morning of the 6th, while he visit the Holy Hill, for the first time he sees Nancy, he approaches to salute her and he semlls a rose fragance and remembers that it is the same one he felt on June 5th in Bolivia.

1 . -

His trip to Conyers is to study, investigate and he wants to know if the Virgen really appears. For nine days he, as a clinical psychology expert with 21 years of experience, studies and interviews nancy twice. He studies her, does not find any apparent pathologies, as a matter of fact he finds her a very spiritual person, kind, humble, with an immense concern for the goodness of mankind, it seems to him that she has a very transcendental inner life.

On September 11th, Roberto Barbery, a 38 years old bolivian friend arrives. He is an economist and a business manager, who has never been very religious and who wanted to live this experience. On September 13th, together with 17.000 people they go where the apparitions take place. The psychologist's mother has asked him for three rosaries to bring her back to Bolivia. He takes three and while he is putting them away inside his bag, a rose fragance come from it, surprised, he decides to get some more and in each of the four consecutive times, a rose aroma would come out from the interior of the bag.

At 12.00 o'clock on September 13th, songs and prayers begin, suddenly the doctor feels the scent of roses and a second later they hear through the loud speakers that "the Virgen is there".

In this ocassion both visitors went to confession after more than 20 years away from the Catholic Church. They decide to invite Nancy Fowler to visit Bolivia. On this opportunity, the psychologist has taped on a portable tape recorder the Virgen's message. Wishing to sen it to Bolivia, while copying the message, surprisingly, he listens that when the Virgen says: "Stop murdering" (referin to the abortions) children weepings are heard. Afterwards, the Virgen mentions "more disasters will come" and the sound of strong winds and whistling tornados are heard from the tape, even though the 13th was a radiant day and no wind blew at all.

Nancy is invited to visit Bolivia, it is thought by the month of March.

2. ARRIVAL TO BOLIVIA:

After receiving the invitation from the "Group for peace", with the authorization from the city of La Paz Archbishop Mons. Luis Sainz Hinojosa, Nancy agrees to come to Bolivia on February 28th, in order to address the people from March 1st. through the 5th. In Bolivia, everyone is surprised that the Virgen Mary has appeared in many countries, except in Bolivia.

On the expected day, Nancy arrives with George Collins, who transcribes the messages regularly. Meetings with praying groups have been arranged in centers, churches and one in a scientifical Symposium where the issues of "Aggression and Peace" of modern society are discussed. The people present at this meeting, are above all scholars and many of them non catholics.

Up to March 2nd., the experiences are very normal and natural, Nancy's and George's visit is the one corresponding that of two normal and goodwill persons. On Wednesday the 3th, Nancy narrates how Christ spoke to her on the previous night, she also mentions that she received a message for Bolivia, where it says that in Bolivia there is not forgiveness. Nancy is surprised because on the contrary, she has seen, up to that moment, good people, but the psychologist explains to her that really in this country, people ought to forgive more, ther is a lot of resentment and animosity.

2.-

On Wednesday, something impressive occurs: At the noon Mass, there are 8 persons next to the Priest Ricardo Campos, who is celebrating mass and is spiritual director of the "Group for peace", group which has invited Nancy. During the Mass, Nancy has the vision of Jesus and He tells her that He has "a message for Lucia" (the maid who works for the family where Nancy and George are staying). When the Mass ends, the surprised people presente there, hear that Nancy says the the Maid: "Jesus says that He forgives you all your sins". NO one understands the reason of the message, but in the other hand, it seems obvious for a seer to speak that way ... but the explanation comes afterwards, when the maid says: "Last night when Mrs. Nancy went out, I went intho her bedroom to pray to the Crucified Christ, which she brought, I have prayed and put it on my forehead asking Him to forgive all my sins from the moment I learned to speak" (Lucia is 28 years old). Nancy could not have known this prayer, since Nancy does not speak Spanish, and her contact with Lucia was minimun, and Lucia does not speak English and she speaks the aymaras' Spanish spoken in thes region.

The perfume of roses has impregnated into variosu persons, among them, was a doctor who attende Nancy, a protestant pastor, who after the conversations with Nancy, went for confession to a Catholic priest.

3. THE APPARITION ON MARCH 5th.

On Friday 5th, Nancy was ending her meetings in La Paz, with a conference about "Aggression and Peace", she was addressing to more than 350 scholars of the behavior, health, psychology, education sciences, giving a message of peace from Conyers. Her presence was a success, she ended when a large group of people came close around her and they prayed together.

Returning from the closure of the Symposium, while we were in the dining room at 10.40 p.m., Ramiro 8 years old, and Cynthia 12, together with Lucia 28, were leaving Nancy's bedroom and they asked us if we could see what they were seeing. In the room, hanging from a wall there was a wooden rosary, which was brought from Rome to the owner of the house, but at that moment, its shape and parts were reproduced on the wall like a phosphorescent light that would moved to the whole length, forward, behind, up and down from the wall. Ramiro and Cynthia also saw how Nancy's Crucifix would moved on the wall, too. Cynthia says that when she saw it she was afraid and she grasped Lucia. Lucia told the children to let this be known among the adults present there and who were the following:

- *Nancy Fowler and George Collins,*

- *Nélida Gómez, 77 years old and the children's grandmother,*

- *R.P. Ricardo Campos, SDB., 50, Salesian priest, Don Bosco Primary School Director from the city of La Paz, spiritual director of the "Group for peace",*

- *Johnny Córdova, 35, psychologist,*

- *Natty Rojas, Ramiro's and Cynthia's mother, aerophotographist,*

- *Roberto Barbery, 38, economist and business manager,*

3.-

60

- Dr. Bernardo Marzana, 73 lawyer,

- Lucía Blanco, the Gómez home maid,

- Dr. Ricardo Castañón, 44, clinical psychologist, university professor, neuropsychophysiology researcher,

(Dr. Castañón's statement):

The children, at first, called for their grandmother and all of us, adults, went in to the room where Nancy was staying, we saw all the rosaries in the same shape of the original wooden rosary, with its own phosphorescent light that moved on the wall height and wide lenght wise, from left to right, and so did all of the other religious objects that were hanging form the wall. While the group was in the stat of admiration and surprised, Nancy walke in and spoke directly: *"Oh angel Michael, your are here, ¿what are you doing?"* the lights increased and I observed some horizontal lights that came out form the Virgen's feet. At this moment Nancy said: *"Bring the Virgen from the other room, because the Holy Virgen will appear, put her on the TV"* (it was the only high place where the statue of the Virgen could be put). Due to the fact I spoke English and understood Nancy's request, I obeyed her request and placed the image on the TV, since it was the only hight place in the room and Nancy was looking at that angle, at the ceiling.

All of us knelt down, qhile Nancy was talking with the angel Michael. She said: "Where are many angels who are moving the rosary from this side to the other" (it explained the movements of the rosary). In that instance, probably 10.47, the Virgen (image) was seen by Cynthia with a splendor, noticing that the image got large and then small; Dr. Castañón also saw the same aureola that he already saw and photographed in Conyers.

Nancy stated in that instant: *"The Virgen is appearing"*, the radiance of the statue increased (Dr. Castañón). Nancy in a mystic attitude, looked at the Virgen, verified if it was in reality Her saying: *"If your are not the Sacred Mother, leave"*. The Virgen said this message(*): *"My dear children, I do come in the name of my Son Jesus. I am God's loving mother and your Mother. Please, my children, remove from your hearts your unfogiveness, you must pray a lot"* Nancy comments: *"The Virgen is crying, please do not cry"* (she points our that tears are coming out from her right eye). *"The leaders from this country must not continue hurting the children of God, I please, request to built here an altar. I have come to thank my dear daughter, your work satisfies my son and myself. Did you see the rosary? it is a sign for this country, I request that everyone of my children pick up the Rosary and pray. More difficult times are yet to come for my children of the world. You have to pray a lot my children"*. Nancy talks:*"Oh Mother, I am so happy to see you"*. *"My dear daughter, I thank you. Children, when I leave, I ask you to make the sign of the cross and please do not forget to thank my son for allowing me to come. I love you and I bless you"*. At the end of the message, Nancy says:*"The Virgen is in the ceiling, she is going away, ¡she is gone!"*, and she asked us to pray a rosary.

---

* This is a translation from Spanish into Enghish, from the report given to the Archbishop of La Paz.

4.-

4. SCIENTIFIC STUDIES:

Due to the importance of these events, Dr. Ricardo Castañón requested and suggested Mrs. Nancy Fowler to do some neuropsychophysiological outlines of her.
For this purpose he invited the following professors:

Prof.Dr. Joaquín Arce Lema, neurosurgeon, professor ath the State University of La Paz, and Dr. Carlos Encinas, neurologist, who are encharged for doing the encephalogram; Prof. Emilio Sotomayor, clinical psychologist of the city of Cochabamba; Lic. Margarita Foster, reseracher in Japan and at the moment invited professor at the Bolivian Catholic University, expert in psychodiagnosis and who did not have any knowledge about Nancy. Dr. Castañón provides his office for the studies. A photographer, Lic. Jorge Handal; Dr. Bernardo Marzana filmed and had the assitance of a secretary.

4.1. PSYCHOPHYSIOLOGICAL OUTLINE:

A electromiograph EMG, was used. This instrument measures the electrical discharge of muscular fibers and quantizises the contractions as well as the relaxation. Setting the register electrodes on the frontal area, registered a stress activity of 1.5 and 1.7 microvolts, which indicates a stress status likely due to the tests themselves, which causes ansiety and others. But the importance of this test takes place on the fact that in order to relax down to 0.2 microvolts, usually it takes between 8 to 10 therapeutical working sessions. At the momento when it registered 1.5 - 1.7, Nancy was asked to "atart praying" in that instant, in a thounsath of second, the needle registered 0.2, therefore showing an amazing state of relaxation.

4.2. ELECTROENCEPHALOGRAM:

It was performed by Prof.Dr. Joaquín Arce and by Dr. Carlos Encinas. The results are now being evaluated and they will go through comparative studies to be performed by other experts in the U.S.a., in order to present a complete, general and widely confirmed report. What at the moment it may be informed is that it indicates than Nancy, during the tests, when she was asked to see something "she used to see lights" and in the registry was proven to see something "she used to see lights" and in the registry was proven by the modifications in the EEG outline pattern and when she was asked to see images, the electroencephalografic sketch modified in such a way that it was similar to the one of a person with a lot of muscular activity, which the obervers did not externally see on Nancy. During the visions, this "muscular" registry showed an extraordinary activity that surprised all the experts, because it can not be explained from the point of view of normal cortical activity and neither it explains patholigies related to a similar reaction.

5. TRIP TO COCHABAMBA:

5.-

62

Due to Nancy's visit, the "Centro María Reina de La Paz" and the Archbishop of the city of Cochabamba, invited Nancy to this city where many people benefited from her presence.

In this first visit to Bolivia, more than 3200 people were present at Nancy's encounters in La Paz and Cochabamba, and through TV, at least 10.000 persons became aware of the events in Conyers, Georgia, USA.

At the time, after Nancy's visit we know from a lot of people who began to pray the rosary everyday, some of them visit already praying groups and maney want to live the catholic religion in a better way.

For the report: **"International Center for Human Studies"**
and
"Group for peace"
P.O.Box, SM: 12366
La Paz - Bolivia
Phones: (02) 79 52 64 - (02) 79 58 00

R.P. Ricardo Campos S.D.B.

Prof.Dr. Ricardo Castañón-Gómez

Lic. Roberto Barbery

Dr. Bernardo Marzana

La Paz, april 13, 1993

6.-

Scientific studies on Nancy Fowler abound and continue at this moment. Nancy submitted to more tests on June 13, 1993, conducted in Conyers, Georgia.

On June 13, five scientific teams were present in Conyers along with 80,000 pilgrims. The scientific teams were led by Dr. Ricardo Castañón, Bolivian neuropsychologist. Dr. Ramone Sanchez, an Atlanta neurologist and epilectologist, also participated. Dr. Sanchez is one of a handful of specialists in the world doing this kind of work. Nancy Fowler was found free of any epileptic or psychotic tendencies. The equipment used on Nancy is the most sophisticated and advanced available.

Dr. Sanchez, a believer in Nancy, said the tests revealed a spiritual presence.

Nancy told the doctors to take a reading on the Crucifix in a side room adjacent to the room of apparitions. A heartbeat was detected coming from the glowing Crucifix.

All teams are writing up scientific papers on the apparition. Once again Nancy Fowler has been tested. Dr. Callahan concludes once again that there is no question that apparitions are taking place in Conyers.

The statue of Our Lady in front of Nancy Fowler's home. Pilgrims leave petitions, flowers, and rosaries here.

Taken Christmas '92, these photos of Our Lady of Fatima show the lifelike features which the statue assumes. Note especially the hair and the eyes' pupils. (Photo by Rick Green)

Janie McIsaac, Mona Karam, and the author by the miraculous statue of Our Lady of Fatima. Note the texture of the statue, which is an opaque, "space-age" plastic with no shadows or lifelike features.

Thousands patiently wait on the 13th of each month for a visit from Mary.

On any given day, crowds gather at the Holy Hill to pray.

Chip Hancock at the well containing alleged healing water blessed by Jesus. Pilgrims collect water in background.

The Crying Statue at the Holy Hill.

The sky with a silhouette of Our Lady, taken at Conyers on May 13, 1992, the 75th anniversary of Fatima. (Photo by Betty March)

Joan Cashon from New York in the room of apparitions, just before giving testimony about her cancer (left), and (right) during testimony (February, 1993).

Margaret (right) and Mary Margaret, in front of Holy Spirit Monastery, October 14, 1991. (Photo by Jack Smith)

An unusual funnel cloud, shot on May 13, 1993 by writer John Maloney of *Style Weekly*.

The sky on Apparition Day. (Photo by David Lukes)

The sky around noon on Sept. 13, 1992. (Photo by Nancy Placek)

Apparition Day, Sept. 13, 1992.
(Photo by Al Placek)

The embryo appears in the sky
(Sept. 13, 1992). (Photo by Nancy Placek)

The sky as it appeared on the Feast of the Immaculate Conception (December 8. 1992). Pilgrims often report that everything becomes bathed in a golden light. (See Carol Bradford's testimony.)

In the light over the farm house on the 13th of each month, the image of the Blessed Mother could be seen. (Photo by David Lukes)

Nancy Fowler prays with a boy as double circles of light engulf them. (Photo by Patty Copsey)

Steps and the light leading
to the Sun as Mary
departs, Nov. 13, 1992.
(Photo by Eleanor Ripple)

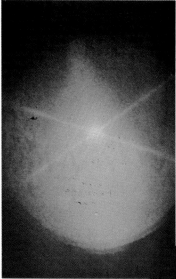

The sun,
photographed on
April 13, 1992.
(Photo by Leslie
Quade)

Miraculous photo
of the Holy Hill at
night. (Photo by
Eleanor Ripple)

The Apparition Room. The Blessed Mother appears in the white corner of the room.

Louis Cashon of New York and James Tsakanikas of Virginia help a handicapped pilgrim in the Room of Apparitions.

Corner of the Apparition Room where the Blessed Mother appears. Visible is a ribbon of Divine Mercy Rays. (Photo by Karen Beherens, Oct. 13, 1992)

Chip and Tom Hancock stand before the simple wooden cross at the farm house. Note that there are no lights in the area.

The simple wooden cross illuminated from within. . .an impossibility. (Photo by James Tsakanikas)

Pilgrims'
cameras often
capture a door
clearly visible in
the sky during
apparitions.

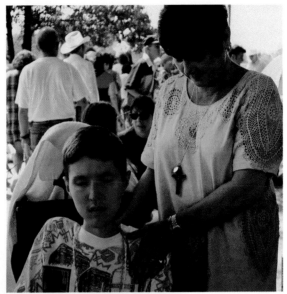

The author, praying with Danny Ward, June 14, 1993. (Photo by Jerrilyn Ward)

Picture of bleeding crucifix taken on Holy Hill on July 13, 1993. Note the wound in the side (circled on photo)).

Nancy Fowler in a casual moment, with her dog, Happy Girl.

Nadia Martinez (on her 5th birthday), with her photo of Blessed Mother, October 13, 1992. (Photo by Lenora Matinez)

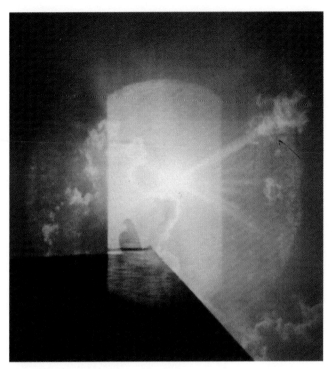

Dove on the roof, taken June 13,
1993, by Joe Mullins.

On the Feast of the
Precious Blood,
June 13, 1993, the
new crucifix
(below) at the Holy
Hill, began to bleed.

Photo of the sky at Conyers taken on
July 13, 1993 by Felipe de La Hoz.

The face of Jesus appeared in this
extraordinary photo shot from a bus window.

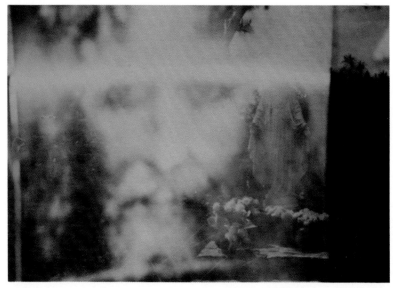

Messages of Jesus and Mary

"I, Jesus, am calling all my children here. It is natural. My Mother would appear here to bring my children to me. My Mother never brings children to herself, unto herself, apart from me."

There have been many messages given by Our Lady and Our Lord at Conyers. Messages fall into two categories—private and public. While Nancy Fowler is visited daily by Our Lord and his Blessed Mother, there are public messages given on the 13th of the month for the United States. These will be shared. For an in-depth listing of messages, please refer to Nancy Fowler's *To Bear Witness That I am the Living Son of God.*

I. There Is Too Little Faith Here (September 2, 1990)

"There is too little faith here. I am very sad. This is my first message for the United States of America." Our Loving Mother said to Nancy that she would appear on the 13th of each month with a message for the United States.

II. Prayers And Sacrifices Are Needed (October 13, 1990)

"Pray much because there is too little prayer from the heart. There is too little prayer." Our Loving Mother looked very sad. She said, *"Your prayers and sacrifices are needed in order to spare you a great punishment from God. My Son's heart is heavily burdened. You will only be able to console Him by giving Him your heart. My dear children, please give my Son your hearts in prayer. Pray, Pray, Pray."*

Our Loving Mother was asked if she had any other messages. She said, *"I encourage family prayer. When you fail to pray in families you will have greater sufferings and Satan will divide. Please, I have come to represent the Holy Family. You are called to imitate us and stay together. Satan seeks greater division in families and countries and church."*

Our Loving Mother held the Baby Jesus in her arms during the whole message.

III. The Appearance in Black (November 13, 1990)
The Blessed Mother, Our Loving Mother, appeared to Nancy in black, but did not speak.

IV. Jesus Explains His Mother's Appearance In Black (November 13, 1990)
Later that afternoon while praying the Rosary, Nancy asked Jesus, "Where is the message for the United States? Where is the Blessed Mother?"

Jesus said, *"My Mother has already given the message. She appeared in black."*

V. Eternal Life With God Is Forever (December 13, 1990)
"I have been sent by God to deliver a message for this country. "My dear children, I wish to teach you this day. Mortal life is short. Eternal life with God is forever. From my motherly heart I mourn for all the lost souls in this country. Pray. Pray. Pray much for the salvation of souls.

"I bless you, and I give you rays of love from my heart. Thank you for responding to my call."

VI. A Nation Given The Most Has Rejected God The Most (January 13, 1991)
"My dear children, please know that I have come as your Loving Mother. I have come to deliver a grave message [she was very, very sad]. *Sorrow reigns in Heaven over the many lost souls in this country. I implore you with a most urgent plea, turn back to God now for sorrow will reign in your land. I am very sad. My children everywhere have ignored my Son. This nation needs a great conversion.*

"I will echo the words of my Son again. A nation, which is given the most, has rejected God the most. I will end by saying I will continue to pray for all of you and continue to beg of my Son's Mercy.

"Thank you for listening to the words of my Son. I am only a messenger from Heaven sent to echo His words to you. Thank you. Please make the sign of the cross as I depart and thank my Son for permitting me to come." Nancy questioned the theology of sorrow reigning in Heaven. On July 22, 1991, she was given an inner locution from the Blessed Mother, *"My Son's Heart reigns in Heaven and His Heart is sorrowful for all the lost souls all over the world."*

VII. Live A Life Of The Soul (February 13, 1991)
"I invite my children to be comfortable. I will give a message for the United States. My dear children of America, as your Loving

66

Mother I would like to teach you. Live a life not of the flesh. Live a life of the soul. Your flesh will return to ashes. The life of your soul is forever. Repent and come back to God. Your salvation depends upon this. The war will become worse. There will be more sorrow in families, my dear children. War is a punishment from God. [Nancy said the Blessed Mother was very sad.] *I will remain with you in prayer and I extend my hand to you. Help me to help you to come back to my Son. I bless you. "*

VIII. Without Prayer A Soul Withers and Dies (March 13, 1991)

"The message today is: pray, America, pray. Continue your prayers and sacrifices and offer these to God daily. For the many children who have not yet started on their journey of prayer, I implore you from my motherly heart to start. Without prayer a soul withers and dies. Prayer is your lifeline to God. I come as your Loving Mother and invite you to come out of darkness into the light. I bless you. "

IX. Children of America Take My Hand (April 13, 1991)

"Dear children of America, as your Loving Mother I am calling you. Take my hand and walk with me on a path to my Son. Children of America, take my hand. Many of you are walking on a path away from my Son and you are in danger of losing your life with God forever. Repent and turn back to God. Children, please come. With tears I am pleading with you. I bless you. " [Our Loving Mother was crying while she was pleading.]

X. Are You Prepared To Meet The King? (May 13, 1991)

"My dear children, prepare the way for my Son. Are you ready to greet Him? He will come in an hour you do not know. Shouldn't you be prepared to meet the King? Live a life of holiness. Walk in complete faith and trust. For the many who have gone astray, please turn from your sinful ways and return to God. Do not be deceived by the lures of this world's kingdom. The kingdom of God and the kingdom of this world do not mix. Pray, children, pray. As your Loving Mother I am calling you to God. I bless you. Thank you. "

XI. Please, Stop Offending God (June 13, 1991)

"Please, children of America, stop offending God. Do not think that punishment will not come. I am pleading with you to come back to my Son. Do not delay. The time is now. Our hearts are grieving. Please, children of American, I am calling you to my Son. As your Loving Mother, I bless you. "

XII. Make Your Hearts Ready (July 13, 1991)

"My dear children of America, where are your hearts? Prepare your hearts by opening your hearts to My Son. Preparation is a time to get ready. Be ready. Throughout your life, you are getting ready for work, for appointments, for leisure, for rest. Make your hearts ready. If your heart is closed, My Son remains on the outside, knocking. Open your heart. Be clean. My Son is waiting to give you gifts. As your Loving Mother, I bless you—and bless each other."

XIII. Desire Peace (August 13, 1991)

"My dear children of America, today I come among you to deliver an invitation of peace. Desire peace in yourselves, in your families, in your communities and in countries. Peace comes only when you are united to my Son. Apart from my Son there is no peace."

At this point Nancy said, "She is crying and there is a stream of light going down her cheek as if a tear."

"Children of America, your refusal of my Son's peace will bring greater suffering upon you."

Nancy said, "She is crying again. Another stream of light streamed down her cheek like a tear."

"Please, [as if pleading] amend your lives and return to God. As your Loving Mother, I bless you."

XIV. Make A Decision To Love God And To Stand In Faith (September 13, 1991)

"My dear children of America, make a decision to love God and to stand in faith. The days are rapidly approaching when your faith will be greatly tested. Be strong in my Son.

"Children, you must stop offending God for greater sufferings are awaiting you. Do not think that a punishment will not come. Please stop offending my Son.

"Return to God and keep His laws. As your Loving Mother, I bless you and I'm blessing everything you brought with you.

"That is the end of the message for the United States."

XV. Put God First In Your Life (October 13, 1991)

"My dear children of America, today I come among you on the anniversary of my visits here. I come in the name of my Son, Jesus. This is a time for reflection and renewal. Reflect upon the words of my Son. Renew your commitment to put God first in your life. Put your life in order. Pray, America, pray. Please make consecrations to our hearts. As your Loving Mother, I bless you and send rays of love from my motherly heart."

Nancy said Our Loving Mother grew more radiant and a crown

appeared above her head.

"With outstretched arms, I pour forth graces upon you. That is the end of my message for the United States."

XVI. Please, Children, Unless You Amend Your Lives, My Son's Hand Is About To Strike (November 13, 1991)

"My dear children of America, are you listening? Are your ears closed or open? Are your hearts closed or open? Think about the goodness of God. Be thankful."

Nancy said a tear came out of both her eyes. Out of one came something thicker.

"Please, children, unless you amend your lives, my Son's hand is about to strike. As your Loving Mother, I bless you."

XVII. I Bring Gifts Of Peace And Good Will (December 13, 1991)

"My dear children of America, as your Loving Mother I bring gifts of peace and good will to you. Open these gifts by opening your hearts. Be prayerful and be imitators of God's good will. Children, your births are gifts from God. Let the life of God live in you. Reject and hate sin. Children, I give you my Son. He is the Prince of Peace and God of Good Will." Nancy said that she had her hands stretched as she said, *"Proclaim Emmanuel. I bless you dear children. As you make the sign of the cross, I will depart. Remember to thank my Son for permitting me to come. I love you dear little children."*

XVIII. You Cannot Love God Without Keeping His Commandments (January 13, 1992)

"Dear children of American, be children of light. Walk away from sin. Please children, many of you are in danger of losing Heaven forever. There is no greater suffering than the loss of God. Prepare yourselves for eternal happiness. Come follow my Son's light. Banish all darkness from your souls. Keep the laws of God. You cannot love God without keeping His commandments. I bless you. I am praying for you to come to the light. As my Son went to the water for His Baptism, I ask you to return to the light of your Baptism. Please remember to thank my Son for allowing me to come."

XIX. Know The Commandments of God (February 13, 1992)

"Dear little children of America, it is a grace to desire simpleness and littleness. Ask for the grace to live simply and to be humble. Be children of light. Know the commandments of God and carry these laws of God in your hearts. In this way you will know God and you will grow in love with Him and with each other. Little children, the

commandments of God have been given to you to help you be united with God. My Son and I love each of you. I desire each of you to be united with my Son forever. Please amend your lives and return to God. Please do as I ask, or you will have much more to suffer. I bless you. Come and seek refuge in my Immaculate Heart. I am Blessed Virgin Mary the Loving Mother of God, and your Loving Mother. Come little children, and let me lead you to my Son. As you make the sign of the cross, I will bless you and everything you have brought with you. Please thank my Son for permitting me to come. "

XX. Carry Your Crosses And Follow In My Son's Footsteps (March 13, 1992)

"Dear Children of America, please understand these times are times of great mercy. The cup of salvation overflows upon the United States and over the whole world. Bathe, little children, in the love and mercy of God. Be clean. If you refuse the love and mercy of God and refuse to be clean, then greater sufferings will befall you. Prepare. Deny yourself. Carry your cross and follow in my Son's footsteps. He has set the path before you. Unless you are following in His footsteps, you are not following. Live for God. Walk the passion in Love. Let me help you each step of the way.

"Thank you, my dear little children. This is the end of the message. "

XXI. America, Awaken From Your Sleep (April 13, 1992)

"Dear Children of America, with tears I plead with you. Pray, children, pray. Begin your journey of prayer by taking a step. Examine your relationship with God and with each other. Amend your life. Please listen. You will suffer much more by living apart from God. At this time meditate upon the passion of my Son, Jesus, and in this way you will receive the strength for the passions of your life. America, awaken from your sleep and stand with my Son. I bless you and I love you. "

XXII. America, Join Hands With Each Other (May 13, 1992)

"Dear Children of America. There is great joy in my heart to come among you, my dear children, on this anniversary of my appearance in Fatima. Seventy-five years ago I came to Portugal requesting prayers and sacrifices in reparation for the for the sins of the world. Today I come with the same request.

"Little children, listen with your hearts. I plead with you. Shield your heart in mine. Please, children, I ask you to make consecration to my Immaculate Heart and in this way I can protect you. As your Loving Mother, I desire each of you to receive the help that you seek

from God as He wills. God favors the petitions of His little ones. Be humble before God and each other. Let the peace of God live in your hearts, in your families and in this land. I bless you. Desire the love and peace of God and live His love and peace. America, join hands with each other. "

XXIII. The June 13, 1992, Monthly Message

"Dear Children of America, please forgive one another. When you fail to forgive, you fail in love. Your sins are many. Please children, you must stop offending God who is grievously offended. When you remain in serious sin, you risk losing your soul. You allow Satan to guide you. Walk away from the darkness of sin. [Nancy said at this point that the Blessed Mother was radiant.] *Come to the light of truth. Satan is deceiving you and you do not recognize him. The darkness over this land will grow darker and you will have more suffering unless you return to God. "* [Nancy saw a thick, very dark substance like blood come out of the Blessed Mother's eye.]

XXIV. The July 13, 1992, Monthly Message

"My dear little child, darkness is over America and more darkness will come unless you return to my Son. Satan has infiltrated every aspect of your life. Recognize him and free yourself of him. [Nancy saw everything bursting in light. Edwin saw it as well.] *Please listen to these words with your heart. Follow my Son; His way is Life. This message is for everyone in every walk of life. Children, please heed these words. I bless you. At this time you may hold the articles you brought with you and I will bless them. Please tell my children I've received the petitions of your hearts and I've brought them to my Son. Please make the sign of the cross as I depart. (Nancy, you will not be able to see me at this time). Remember to thank my Son. "*

XXV. The August 13, 1992, Monthly Message

"Dear Children of America, each person is my precious little child. As your Loving Mother, I love you with unconditional love. I come in the name of my Son, Jesus. Please little children, cooperate with God's plan of salvation. My Son shows you the way of salvation. Follow Him. Help me to help you. With God, together let us push the cloud of darkness away from this country. [A tear then rolled out of her eye.] *Begin where you are and pray. The time will come when God's mercy will change into God's justice and the greatest suffering will befall you. Do not delay in coming to my Son. This is an urgent plea for all mankind. I bless you. Please make the sign of the cross as I depart. At this time everything is being blessed. Remember to thank my Son for permitting me to come. "*

XXVI. The September 13, 1992, Monthly Message

"Dear Children of America, are you listening? Are you listening with your hearts? Many of you have started on a spiritual journey and many of you have stopped. Do not allow Satan to discourage you. Believe with your whole heart in My Son. Allow My Son to lead you. My children, pray and offer sacrifices for the souls of your sisters and brothers. Pray and offer sacrifices for peace. I implore you to walk away from the sins of the flesh. Stop murdering. There are grave consequences if you continue to ignore God and violate His laws. It is a great grace that God has permitted me to come. I love you and I desire each of you to be united to My Son. More disasters are coming. [She cried. Blood came out of her eye.] *Please listen. Look at the way you are living. Look within yourself and examine your relationship with God and amend your life without delay. I bless you. As you make the Sign of the Cross, I will depart. Remember to thank My Son for permitting me to come."*

XXVII. The October 13, 1992, Monthly Message

"Dear Children of America, there is great joy in My heart to see you gathered in prayer. There is great sorrow in My heart for many of My children are lost. Many children do not pray and they have closed their ears to the messages of God. [Nancy saw a tear of blood coming down the side of her nose.] *Pray, children, pray. Prayer is vital. Seventy-five years ago I came to three little shepherd children to deliver a message to all mankind and I have come today to deliver a message. Children, you must stop offending God. Begin with this anniversary day and make a commitment to spend time with God every day.* [Nancy said Our Loving Mother is crying again.] *Pray the Rosary every day. I ask that you make an act of consecration to the Sacred Heart of My Son and My Immaculate Heart. In our hearts you will find a safe refuge.*

"America, raise your voices in great thanksgiving to God for His mercy, for his love. I cannot restrain My Son's hand. Please help me to help you. Offer your daily sacrifices and prayers, please, in reparation for the sins of the world. Keep Our messages alive in your hearts.

"Join your hands and your hearts with God and with each other. With your hands and hearts joined, please pray the Our Father. [With hands joined, all the pilgrims prayed the Our Father.] *Please, remember this prayer is given to you by My Son.*

"I will bless you and I will bless everything you have brought with you. Please make the sign of the cross as I depart. From My Immaculate Heart I give rays of love. Always remember to thank My Son."

XXVIII. The November 13, 1992, Monthly Message

"Dear Children of America, with tears I plead with you. Do not throw away the commandments of God. A nation apart from God will suffer more and will fall deeper into darkness. Please children, pray for your leaders and for this Country. You will be stripped of your pride and you will be purified. Children, I love you. Please pray and be united in God."

XXIX. The December 13, 1992, Monthly Message

"Dear Children, COME! Come, little children, give your heart to My Son. Adore, praise and thank Him for His endless love and mercy. God has given you many signs. You fail to recognize the hand of God in everything. God has not separated Himself from you. You have chosen to live apart from Him. When you follow false gods, you emit more darkness into the world. Our hearts are bleeding for you. With My Son, together let us push the darkness away. I have warned you about war and, again, I warn you about war. Pray and sacrifice for peace, please. I warned you about disasters. Again, I warn you about more disasters. Pray and sacrifice, please. I love you, My dear little children. I desire to shield you in My Immaculate Heart. Reform your heart and let the love of My Son grow in each of your hearts." [Nancy said, "She is so radiant!"]

"Children, I will bless you now and everything you have brought with you and remember to thank My Son for permitting Me to come. [Nancy said, "She smiled a little."] *As you make the Sign of the Cross, I will bless you and everything you brought with you and I will depart."*

XXX. The January 13, 1993, Monthly Message

"My dear children, as your Loving Mother, I ask you from the tenderness of My heart, are your ears blocked and are your hearts closed to the word of God? My Son has sent me to help you. Many of you refuse to believe that I speak the words of My Son. Children, please, I have warned you about more disasters. [Nancy said the Blessed Mother was crying.] *I have warned you about war and I have asked for your help but you refuse to listen. Unless you amend your ways and pray, in a weakened state you will fall to your knees. Children, I love you and I desire each of you to be united with My Son. My Son's hand is rich in love and mercy. It is about to be turned to the hand of justice.* [Nancy saw blood or something thick come out of the Blessed Mother's left eye.] *Pray, children, pray. Your hearts will be purified. See the love and mercy of My Son in everyone, in everything. Let it be foremost always.*

"At this time I will bless you and everything you have brought with

you. As you make the Sign of the Cross, I will depart. I will depart yet I will remain with you. Please children, remember to thank My Son. Again, I ask for your prayers and sacrifices. "

XXXI. The February 13, 1993, Monthly Message
"My dear children, please quiet your hearts. I ask you to stop right where you are. Thank about God more and talk to Him more.

"Many of you will find these instructions too basic. Many of My children are infants and are very young. Many, many of you have not taken your first step on your journey back to God. Please understand My Son has sent Me to help you. Take My hand. Take My heart and listen. God's plan for each of you is to know Him and to grow in Love. This time is your time. Each soul is unique unto God and God has given each soul a unique journey. Grow, little children, in Love. I bless you.

"As you make the Sign of the Cross, I will depart yet I will remain with you wherever you pray. [The face of Jesus appeared momentarily.] Please remember to thank My Son. "

XXXII. The March 13, 1993, Monthly Message
"My dear children, with tears from my Immaculate Heart I plead with you. Children, you must come out of your cities of darkness and come into the light. My Son is looking upon the cities of the world and weeping over many of them.

"Children, you must not offend God any longer. More hardships are coming to My children. I am sorry from My motherly heart to have to tell you these things. I thank you for enduring the hardships and sacrifices.

"Everyone has received My special blessing this day and all who have desired to be here have received the same blessing.

"I love you, dear little children. Please come back to God while there is still time.

"I am blessing you and all you have brought with you. I am blessing all those who have desired to be here and everything they had with them. Please remember to thank My Son as I depart and please make the Sign of the Cross. "

XXXIII. The April 13, 1993, Monthly Message
"My dear children of America and children of the whole world, rejoice in the Risen Lord. Believe in the Resurrection wholeheartedly. You are called to be believing people of God.

"Pray every day to have the grace of greater faith. Please, children, My Son Jesus is living and you fail to see His living presence everywhere.

"You have chosen to become a slave. You are held in the bondage *of sin. My Son offers you FREEDOM. Come to Him and receive new Life. He is the Way, the Truth, the Life.* [Our Loving Mother was glowing in light.] *He is the Resurrection.*

"My Easter message to each of you is to come to My Son and stay close to Him. Pray more, dear children. Only in Him do you receive your strength that will sustain you in troubled times. It is a great grace from God that My Son has permitted Me to come to you. Please thank Him.

"At this time, My children, I will bless you and everything that you brought with you. You may hold the objects up if you want to. As you make the Sign of the Cross, I will depart. Remember My Son and I are always with you. "

XXXIV. The May 13, 1993, Monthly Message
"Dear children of America, the time has come for you to respond to Our invitations of love. Please, children, wake up while there is still time. You are going deeper and deeper into darkness. Again I say to you: if you refuse the peace of My Son, then you will be at war. You will have war between nations, in your communities, in your families and within yourself.

"On this anniversary day, I ask each of you to recommit your life to God. My children everywhere, join your hands and your hearts to God and to each other.

"Now I will bless you and everything you have with you. I give you My special blessing from My heart. When you make the Sign of the Cross, I will depart yet I will remain with you. "

MESSAGES ON ABORTION

THE MOST IMPORTANT PERSON ON EARTH

"The most important person on earth is a mother. She cannot claim the honor of having built Notre Dame Cathedral. She need not. She has built something more magnificent than any cathedral—a dwelling for an immortal soul, the tiny perfection of her baby's body.

"The angels have not been blessed with such a grace. They cannot share in God's creative miracle to bring new saints to Heaven. Only a human mother can. Mothers are closer to God the Creator than any other creatures. God joins forces with mothers in performing this act of creation. . .

"What on God's good earth is more glorious than this: to be a mother? "

Joseph Cardinal Mindszenty

People often ask why the Holy Mother is appearing in black. She is clearly calling all children back to God. She has been sent by her Son. One of the most important messages relates to abortion. We are reminded of Deuteronomy 30:19, *"I call heaven and earth to witness this day, that I have set before you life and death, blessing and cursing. Choose therefore life, that both thou and they seed may live."*

The Blessed Mother said on October 13, 1992, *"The mothers' wombs have become concentration camps of the world."* She was even more direct on October 15, 1992, when She said, *"Abortion is murder."*

I have suffered many times when I hear young girls or women proclaim, "It's *my* body, I can do as I choose." Can we? Are these bodies ours? Do they belong to us?. . .or. . .are they loaned to us by God? If we are made in the image and likeness of God, then our bodies are temples of the Holy Spirit. Do we have the right to rationalize our behavior and adopt our own agendas?

The Blessed Mother said on September 12th, *"God alone has the right to call souls home. The murders must stop."* Once again, the question remains, "Will we choose to be lights or will we remain in darkness?"

Here below is a listing of Our Loving Mother's messages regarding abortion:

"The blood of My slaughtered unborn will fall upon the United States."
(November 10, 1992)

Jesus said to Nancy, *"I am Jesus who speaks to you. I desire to give you a message.*

"My American children are going to suffer for the sins of abortion and for the rejection of My Commandments. The blood of My slaughtered unborn will fall upon the United States.

"Many of My children are concerned about preparation. The most important preparation is for the soul. Do not get sidetracked with material worldly concerns. Do you not know that I am the giver of gifts? Have you forgotten or do not know that I can multiply?"

The Blessed Mother then spoke and said, *"America, if you stand for murder, you stand against My Son. Abortion is murder."*

Jesus then said, *"America, you will be purified of these sins."*

"Do not put your laws in front of Mine"
(October 15, 1992)

Jesus said, *"Children, know that I am God and love you with an unconditional love. When will you acknowledge that I am God? When will you return love to Me? How long must I wait? I say to all mankind, you are running out of time; I am not. Amend your life and keep My commandments sacred. Do not put your laws in front of Mine. Seek My forgiveness and My mercy.* " [Nancy said Jesus was crying.]

"When you kill the life that He created, then you do not stand with Him. "
(November 13, 1992)

Jesus said, *"My Mother echoes My words. My children should too. "*
Later during the monthly apparition, the Blessed Mother said, *"America must not go the way of man. "*
Nancy saw the pictures in the room of the Sacred Heart of Jesus and the Immaculate Heart of Mary burst into radiant light. Nancy then saw a black light behind the Blessed Mother and asked Her why.
"There is darkness over America. "
Nancy again saw the black light and the Blessed Mother crying. Blood was coming out of Her eye. There was a constant flow of blood out of Her left eye and water out of Her right eye.
"My children are not listening. My children are not listening. "
Nancy asked the Blessed Mother why She kept crying.
"I cry over My slaughtered children. Let My children know I am crying because the children of God are murdered and My children think they are right with God. My Son is life. When you kill the life that He created, then you do not stand with Him. " Nancy saw the Blessed Mother crying continuous streams of blood.

"The mother's wombs have become concentration camps of the world. "
(October 13, 1992)

During the Rosary, Nancy saw a flash a vision of the evil face of Hitler. The Blessed Mother then said, *"The mothers' wombs have become concentration camps of the world. "*
Later the Blessed Mother said, *"A hammer will pound the earth like an angry parent pounds the table. When will you listen? And all the time the parent is loving the child. "*

"When you reject life of the unborn, Satan is attacking and influencing you. "
(November 1, 1992—Feast of All Saints)

77

Nancy said to Jesus, "It is not easy to try to be a saint."

Jesus said, *"It is not easy. It was not easy for Me. A servant is not greater than the Master.*

"Walking in My footsteps is the way to paradise. Walking in My footsteps is not easy but it is the way to life eternal with Me. I have gone before you to prepare a place for you. I walk each step of the way with you. Embrace Me each step of the way. My Mother is with you. She is there for you.

"Children, please do not reject Us for if you do you are pushing away the help that you need. The road is rough and rocky. You will grow weary. You will thirst. I am here with My Mother to help you.

"Children, read the Scriptures and you will find life and strength and all the help that you need in My words. My word is life.

"You were asking Me about Satan. He, the evil one, will distract you in every way to keep you from feeding on My words, to keep you from hearing Me, to keep you away from Me.

"The road is rocky and rough and Satan will distract you in your suffering. Children, when you despair in your suffering, know that Satan has succeeded in keeping you far from Me. The evil one knows when you come to Me you will receive all that you need. So he continually tries tirelessly to keep you far from Me. It is up to you to keep your eyes, your ears, your thoughts, your works, your actions, your every moment on Me.

"If there were not a battle, how would I know your love for Me? Be victorious as the saints were victorious by remaining close to Me. I, the giver of life, have given you the Sacraments to help you. Stay close to Me. Look at the ways in your life and the many times you can reject life. Know that and understand that Satan will attack you by causing you to reject life.

"When you reject life of the unborn, Satan is attacking and influencing you. When you reject the life of Me in the Eucharist, Satan is attacking you and influencing you. When you reject life in My word, Satan is attacking you and influencing you.

"Reflect upon all the areas of your journey towards Me and all the ways that Satan can attack life and know that without My help you will fail. Come to Me often. Stay close to Me and you will have all the help you need.

"You wondered why I took you to Hell again. You must tell My children Hell is a reality that they must know it awaits those who reject life. [Recently, Jesus showed Nancy in a vision both Heaven and Hell.] *I am the way, the resurrection, the life. Guard your words, your thoughts and your actions. Keep pure and desire holiness which is oneness with Me.*

"Thank you for being a listener and a scribe.

"I am the eternal one. I was born of the Holy Virgin Mary. I suffered, died and was buried. I am the resurrection and I stand with My Father and I bow down to My Father. "

Nancy said the light around the crucifix upon which Jesus appeared got very bright and then the crucifix was bursting in light.

"Stop murdering. There are grave consequences if you continue to ignore God and violate His laws. "
(September 13, 1992)

"Dear children of America, are you listening? Are you listening with your hearts? Many of you have started on a spiritual journey and many of you have stopped. Do not allow Satan to discourage you. Believe with your whole heart in My Son. Allow My Son to lead you. My children, pray and offer sacrifices for the souls of your sisters and brothers. Pray and offer sacrifices for peace. I implore you to walk away from the sins of the flesh. Stop murdering. There are grave consequences if you continue to ignore God and violate His laws. It is a great grace that God has permitted Me to come. I love you and I desire each of you to be united to My Son. More disasters are coming. [She cried. Blood came out of Her eye.] *Please listen. Look at the way you are living. Look within yourself and examine your relationship with God and amend your life without delay. I bless you. As you make the Sign of the Cross I will depart. Remember to thank My Son for permitting Me to come. "*

"Abortion is murder. "
(October 13, 1992)

Nancy and a friend were discussing the Blessed Mother's words on abortion in the October 13th monthly apparition: *"The mothers' wombs have become the concentration camps of the world. "* As they talked Nancy saw the Blessed Mother appear many times dressed in black with the Baby Jesus covered with a black cloth. The Blessed Mother was crying as She said, *"When will My children stop murdering; when will they listen?*

"I've come to tell you the mothers' wombs have become concentration camps of the world. Let these words be echoed all over the world. Why are My children not crying? Why are too few of My children concerned? [Nancy said she was crying.] *"Please tell My children of the world the slain babies' blood will be poured out upon the whole world.* [Nancy again said that she was crying.]

How can a mother look in her child's eyes and not feel the hurt when babies are being murdered all around the earth? Let Me repeat

My words you have heard before, dearest daughter, abortion is murder. "

Nancy said, "I see the Blessed Mother's face, then Jesus' face, then the Blessed Mother's face."

"My Son's hand will continue to pound the earth until you stop. Stop violating the laws of God. "

Nancy was crying and said, "Oh Mother, it hurts me that you are so sad."

"Your tears sooth My wounds, dearest daughter. " Nancy said she was crying.

"I am Blessed Virgin Mary. I am the Immaculate Conception. I am the Mother of God and your mother. This is an urgent cry from Heaven. Now make the Sign of the Cross as I depart. "

"The blood of abortions will fall upon mankind. "
(September 30, 1992)

Nancy and friends were praying the Rosary when Nancy saw a vision of a pool of blood at the foot of the cross.

Jesus appeared and said, *"More suffering will befall mankind. The blood of abortions will fall upon mankind. "*

"The sins of abortion are calling forth the wrath of God upon all humanity "
(September 29, 1992)

At morning Mass, Nancy saw an all-black embryo appear on the wall behind the altar. She then saw a life-size profile of the Blessed Mother dressed all in black. Jesus said, *"This is a grave sign. "*

After Mass, Nancy was reading words from Revelation Chapter 12 when Jesus said, *"Don't forget to write those words. "* Jesus was specifically referring to the words: *"Now salvation and power have come; the reign of our God and the authority of Christ are at hand. "*

Later, Nancy and friends were praying the Rosary in the Apparition Room at Nancy's home. The Blessed Mother appeared and Nancy said that She was crying.

The Blessed Mother said, *"Go deeper into the ground for purer water. The day is coming when large amounts of the earth's water will be contaminated. Put a crucifix over the well.*

"Many more diseases will befall mankind. Many will perish. I cannot hold My Son's hand back. Children, pray, please! "

"The day will come when I will tell you to connect the well [to Nancy's house]. *Trust God. "*

Nancy saw something appear on the Blessed Mother's forehead. Nancy asked what it was.

"The same that is on your forehead. It is the cross.

"Many who live by the dollar shall perish by the dollar.

"The sins of abortion are calling forth the wrath of God upon all humanity. Children, children please, please stop murdering."

Nancy said the Blessed Mother was crying blood.

"Children, I love you. I am your Mother.

"America, pick up your Rosary. Kneel down and pray."

Nancy said, "She is crying and crying and crying."

"To My children of the world I say: pray. Pray the Rosary. Pray. Thank you."

"He alone has the right to call souls home."
"The murders must stop."
(September 12, 1992)

While at Mass at St. Pius Church, Nancy heard the Blessed Mother speak: *"Nancy, My little daughter, please write these words. The murders must stop. There are grave consequences if My children do not stop murdering. God is the creator of life. He alone has the right to call souls home. When you violate God's law and murder, you are murderers and gods unto yourselves. You will be banished forever from God unless you stop and repent.*

"Pray about your leaders. Pray they will be and are people of God. If you elect them and they create laws against God, then you will be held accountable."

Nancy asked, "What if you don't know or they change while in office?"

"Then you will be held accountable for what you know at the time of your decision."

Later in the Mass, Nancy saw a vision of an angel appear several times with a dove above its head. She tested the vision and it remained. Jesus said, *"Be assured the angel is from Me."*

After the Mass, Jesus said, *"The murders must stop."*

"The cup of salvation will turn into
the cup of wrath unless you stop."
(March 13, 1992)

The Blessed Mother said, *"My children are not carrying their crosses. My children are murdered all over the world. Tell the people of the United States, tell the people of the world, abortion is murder. The cup of salvation will turn into the cup of wrath unless you stop. Please listen."* [The infant Jesus was now glowing in her arms.]

**"Woe be My people who march with the murderers,
the abortionists. "**
(March 22, 1991)

Jesus said, *"Be patient, bear everything for Me.*
"Many souls are freely choosing to live in darkness. They think their decision is just for a few years on earth but it is for all eternity. Many souls are plunging into eternal fires and are damned for all times. Most are there because of sins of the flesh. Those who willfully choose to murder are there with them.

"Repeated willful impure thoughts, words and deeds are sending people to eternal fires of darkness. My children are making a conscious decision to break My commandment. They repeat this sin then rationalize it and, then, no longer recognize it as sin. I will banish these souls from My sight. I am a God of mercy and love and a just judge. Violation of My commandments kills the life of the soul.

"Woe be to this wicked, sinful generation. How quick you are to cease your prayers of peace the moment you think your peace is achieved. The anger of God the Father is mounting. Woe be My people who march with the murderers, the abortionists. Woe be My priests who engage in impure acts. You have seen enough. You have heard enough. I have spoken. "

**"Unless the murders stop, I will send
a punishment upon this Nation. "**
(March 21, 1991)

At the consecration of the Mass, Jesus said, *"Unless the murders stop, I will send a punishment upon this Nation. "*

Earlier, Jesus said, *"Let Me see this nation, this president, appreciate My mercy and My love. Put God back in this country. Put God back in your schools, in your government, in your leaders, in every man, woman and child. Then, and only then, will you be one great nation under God.*

"I abhor the murders in this land. You have murdered the unborn. You have murdered the word of God, removing it from your schools and your hearts. Put Me back where I belong. "

"Stop trying to be greater than Me."
(January 17, 1991)

Jesus said, *"I have a message for all mankind. Stop trying to be greater than Me. Stop worshiping false gods. Stop murdering. Stop lying. Stop striking Me. Stop ripping My flesh from My bones. Stop ignoring Me. Stop your selfish, egotistical ways. Begin anew. With sincere, repentant hearts turn back to Me. I say to you, love, love, love, every moment, everywhere. Give Me your heart of love. My people need My commandments of love. "*

Earlier the Blessed Mother said, *"Oh, what a terrible, grave sin abortion is.*

"Man continually tries to make decisions that are reserved for God alone. Man does not know the destiny of each child conceived, does not know the destiny of any child conceived. So popes are murdered. Priests are murdered. Nuns are murdered and on and on and on. Does this grave sin not bring about the wrath of God?"

"Murder, murder, murder, murder is in their hearts. "
(December 31, 1990)

Jesus invites all to come to His Holy Hill in Conyers, Georgia, as He said to Nancy, *"My children have failed to demonstrate any faith, any trust and do not believe in our visits here. Let Me say this again, I do not appear like this anywhere else on earth. "*

Nancy saw the suffering face of Jesus.

"The time has come for My Justice. My children do not believe in My Justice and they shall see My Justice. I call and I call and I call and My children do not respond. They do not come.

"I call and I call and I call. They block their ears.

"I am giving the greatest graces here outside of My Mass. Nowhere are My graces being poured forth like they are here. Where are My children? Where are My children at the Mass? Where are My children? I tell you, they are seeking their own selfish selves. How much I have tolerated. Every one of My commandments violated, abandoned.

"Murder, murder, murder, murder is in their hearts. They murder the unborn. They murder the born. They murder the old. They murder the young. They murder the well. They murder the disabled. They slander My name, mock Me. Spit on Me. Throw My words away. My precious daughter, you see My suffering face. Look at Me. You see My love. My children, where have they gone? You are ready to speak My words and there is no one here to listen. "

Nancy said, "The suffering [of Jesus], I can hardly bear it."

"I have given grave signs from Heaven. Know they are grave signs. Nancy, I told you I prefer My children to come back to Me in love. "

These messages speak for themselves. No further commentary is needed from this reporter/author.

MORE MESSAGES FROM JESUS

"I am the Lord, your God. Put no one, nothing before Me. I am Love; I am Life; Live in Me, and I give you Life."

"Walk My way. That is Life. Live My words. That is Life..."

"Everything is better when we do it together. The world allows the body to mature alone. When you walk with Me your body and spirit mature together with Me, not apart from Me."

"Please take the cross that God has lovingly given you. The cross is different for each person because no two people walk the same steps."

"Tell My children I will help them carry the cross. If you don't come to Me, you will be crushed by the weight of the cross. No man can carry the cross alone..."

"When no one around you loves you, come to Me. You can be assured of My love..."

"Please, if you accept My love, then how can you reject, ignore, not honor, not love My Mother? I came through My Mother and I want you, dear children, to come through My Mother on your journey back to Me."

"Bring the new ones, the old ones, the lost ones, the rebellious ones, the smart ones, the proud ones, the lame ones, bring them all. I am the One Who Heals."

All the messages are clear and direct, but will we listen? God in his infinite love respects our free will and right to choose Him. Will we choose to be lights?

Testimony to His Love: Spiritual and Medical Miracles

To say I have been overwhelmed by the love of the people I have met in Conyers is an understatement. Words fail me. They cannot begin to express what I feel in my heart. I have asked some of these kind souls to bear witness that Jesus is The Living Son of God and that He desires an intimate relationship with His children. The following testimonies to God are but a handful of what I have been blessed to receive. I will share as many as I can and I humbly thank all the special people who have been kind enough to share their encounters with God and His Loving Mother. I particularly thank the volunteer organization of Our Loving Mother's Children and Joy Guillot. Joy has been an untiring and powerful support to this effort. I love you, Joy.

I will dispense with any unnecessary dialogue between testimonies. They speak for themselves.

Testimony of Michael Bedoya

My name is Michael. I am a 16-year-old boy and I was born and live in New Jersey.

I am very active in sports and most of the time is taken by either practice for one sport or another or by a game.

Although I have been raised loving God, I have not been a "religious person." I love God and I try to be a good Christian, but I did not spend all my time praying or talking about religion. I am a normal teenager who enjoys worldly things as much as the next guy. I do pray every day, and I feel that we must be very close to Jesus and obey his commandments.

In March of this year, I went to Conyers with a bus load of pilgrims that my mother arranged. When I was in Conyers, I did not feel any different from the way I had felt at home, but when we left, I wanted to come back, so although I said that I did not feel any different, a change was taking place.

I started praying more and got more involved in apparitions of the Blessed Mother. In other words, I paid more attention to God.

In June, my mother took another bus of pilgrims and I wanted to go, so she took me. Before we left, we had learned that my father had a tumor in his thyroid and needed an operation. The doctors were not positive about it. They had told my parents that it could be cancer. Because of my father's age and the type of tumor it was, the chances of it not being cancer were very slim.

While we were in Conyers, I prayed for my father's health. During the apparition I felt a lot of peace. I would say that at this point things were changing. I was feeling different, but still could not explain what I was feeling.

I should tell you that my father has never been a religious person. Catholic, a God loving person, yes, but not a "churchgoer." After his operation, he went to Conyers to give thanks to Jesus and the Blessed Mother. You see, my father is convinced (and so are we) that he had cancer and that Jesus cured him. He gave up smoking, goes to church every Sunday (it's a start) and knows that the Blessed Mother appears in Conyers and has appeared in my room. This is one of the many conversions I have witnessed in Conyers.

Nancy Fowler visited my home July 17-19 and the following events took place.

While staying in my room, Nancy saw angels, had a visit from Jesus and from the Blessed Mother.

I met Nancy on the 17th and she immediately told me that she saw Jesus behind me when she looked at me. She also saw light around me. At this point, I did not understand what it all meant. But I was overcome with the need to cry. I didn't know why.

July 18, 1992 Leonia, N.J.

We (my mother, my father, Edwin and I) were sitting in the living room. We were watching a video on Fatima, when Nancy came out of the room and said, "Come quickly, everybody, the Mother of God is appearing in the room!"

We all went into my room and were kneeling and praying the rosary. I don't remember the exact moment during the rosary when I saw her, but I know I saw the Blessed Mother in the corner of the room.

She was dressed in black. I could not see her facial features, all I saw was an oval shape where the face is, and this shape was of light. I did see her dressed in black with her arms stretched out. I thought it lasted only a few seconds, two or three. But my mother, who was in the room, says that between the time I bowed and started crying and the time I said I no longer saw the Blessed Mother, it was more like one-half to one minute.

While I was seeing her, my chest felt like it was burning. The burning went away when I stopped seeing her.

While we were seeing the Blessed Mother, I looked at Edwin and saw a glow over his head and shoulders and the glow followed him when he moved.

During this vision, my first ever, I could not see Our Lady's face, but in my heart I knew she was beautiful.

September 13, 1992 Conyers, Georgia

Yesterday, I was in Nancy's living room praying and I asked the Blessed Mother to allow me to see her again. I asked to see her face this time and to, please, give people a sign of her presence so that people that do not believe would believe.

Today, I was in the Apparition Room in Conyers, when I saw the Blessed Mother appear on the wall behind the statue. I could not see her body, but this time I saw her face. It was very large and I could see her moving her face and blinking very slowly. I then saw a tear come out of her left eye. The tear was dark, at the moment I did not know what it was, then, I realized it was blood. During the vision, I felt very strong chest pains. I decided to leave the room after I could no longer see the Blessed Mother. When I stopped seeing her, my chest went back to normal and I then left the room.

Our Lady has a beautiful, loving face, like no other face I have ever seen.

People outside said that they saw many signs, the sun was spinning and pulsating, some people saw lights in the sky. Many people said that they saw gold dust come down.

September 10, 1992 Leonia, N.J.

While praying the rosary with some friend in my room, I saw the statue come to life. Her eyes were blinking slowly, first one than the other. I closed my eyes and opened them again to make sure it wasn't because of staring and the vision remained. My mother was in the room and she also saw her eyes open and blink.

October 13, 1992

I was asked by Dr. Callahan (Guadalupe scientist) to be in the Apparition Room during the Blessed Mother's visit. I was praying the rosary along with the others, and I saw the Blessed Mother slightly larger than the statue and to the left of the statue. She was holding the baby Jesus in her arms and at one point I saw her raise her arms and move the baby closer to her face. I also saw Angels all over the room. With the

87

angels were what seemed to me to be doves. All I could see was the silhouette of the angels and the doves, but I am sure of what they were.

I would like to tell you about myself now that I have had these experiences.

Many people ask me if I know why I am being allowed to see the Blessed Mother.

I always answer that I think it is because she wants me to tell young people about it. I am an average teenager who lives a normal everyday life. If I can see the mother of God and tell others about it, it will help her get her message of love across. It is a great grace that I do not deserve, but I accept it along with the responsibility of telling people about it.

I know that the Mother of God is appearing in Conyers.

I like to talk to people, adults and young people, and tell them about my experiences that are graces I have received from Jesus and his Mother. I share these graces. I want everyone to know that God is living. That he is not "just in heaven" as many people say, that he is with us and he wants to let us know that he is among us. I want all the young people to not just think about the material things in life, but to live every day with God. When you need something, your health, your peace of mind, etc., the material things are not going to help you, but God *always* will; don't turn your back on him.

Listen to the messages being given to us by the Mother of God. She is trying to help us return to Her Son.

In the world we live today, drugs, alcohol, and violence are all part of our lives in a very active way. We can easily be tempted to turn to any of these things thinking that they will solve our problems. Well, they *are* our problems and we need God to help us resist temptation.

We are young and it is up to us to decide what kind of adults we are going to be. God will let us make the decision, it is up to us to make the right one.

Jesus is living among us, all you need to do to see this is open your heart. Open your heart to Jesus and His Mother.

I opened my heart and the Blessed Mother touched it. It is a beautiful and scary feeling. Scary at first, when you don't understand what is happening to you, but so beautiful after, when you realize that God has allowed His Mother to show you her love for you.

Michael Bedoya
New Jersey

Testimony of Maria Bedoya

My name is Maria Bedoya. I am Michael's mother.

My journey back to the Lord began one night in mid-February of 1992, with a phone call about "a woman who sees the Blessed Mother in Georgia. . ."

For reasons too numerous to get into at this time, twenty-two years ago I stopped attending Mass and following Jesus' teachings. All I can say is that even though it sounds ironic, it was my love for Jesus that made me stop going to Church.

One night in the middle of February, I received a phone call from my mother, whose friend had given her a book about an apparition in Georgia. (*To Bear Witness That I Am the Living Son of God*). Because this book was in English, they wanted me to read it and tell them what it was all about. My initial reaction was "aha, another nut who says she sees the Blessed Mother." But, as I read the book, I kept getting the feeling that it was authentic, that this was not "another nut". . . this woman was for real. How did I know? I have no idea, all I know is that I decided that I would go to Conyers just as soon as I could.

When I called the airlines, hotels, car rentals, etc., I found that a trip to Conyers on the 13th was more expensive than I could afford. So, I gave up on the idea, but only for a short time. I then thought I could pull it off by renting a bus and getting enough people to come with us. This way, the expenses could be shared as a group and I could get group rates.

My mother and her friend agreed to help me get the people (45) if I organized the entire pilgrimage. The unseen hand of God was busy at work.

The next day, I had hotel rooms, meals, a bus, and everything we needed to go, except for a few details: where are we going? once we get there, what can we expect? what do I tell these 45 people about Conyers? This was clear case of the blind leading the blind. However, I was determined to go to Conyers and meet this woman. I must say that I never thought of seeing anything, I just wanted to go there and meet Nancy.

A few days before the trip was to take place, I called Nancy's home (expecting to have difficulties speaking with her directly) and to my amazement, Nancy answered the phone herself. I asked her a few questions about the apparitions, and what to do once I got to Conyers with a bus full of people. Nancy was very pleasant, very helpful and most of all, as I spoke with her, a feeling of warmth and peace came over me.

After having to overcome a number of obstacles, on March 12, 1992, we were on our way to Conyers. By now, as you may have guessed, God is busy working on my soul, but I wasn't about to go to Church yet.

Our pilgrimage to Conyers went better than expected. In all the excitement, I had left the directions to Conyers at home. Once we were in the Atlanta area, after traveling 16 hours, I realized that I did not have a clue as to where to go now to get to Conyers. All I could remember was that there was Rt. 20 (East or West?) and we had to take one of the three exits to Conyers (which one?) then go to 2324 White Road. Great directions, right?. (At least I remember the entire address.) The bus drivers were very patient with me and we decided to "play it by ear." After getting on Rt. 20 East (we were guessing) we had to guess which exit.

You guessed it, we not only took the right exit, but once on it, we made the right turn to the farm.

Shortly after noon, I felt "heat" coming down from the sky. I started to cry for no apparent reason, and I felt more peaceful than I had ever felt in my life. A few minutes later, a voice said "the Blessed Mother is here." The prayer stopped and the message was given, I knew then that the Blessed Mother was appearing there, I felt it deep inside. The entire trip was like a spiritual retreat. I was convinced that Jesus and his Mother were appearing to Nancy Fowler, even though I did not see anything supernatural, and I did not get the opportunity to speak with Nancy.

We returned to New Jersey and I couldn't wait to go back to Conyers. I planned my next pilgrimage for June. I started to pray the Rosary daily and my life took a different direction.

In June, we returned to Conyers, with another bus of pilgrims. When we were traveling home, the entire bus witnessed the sun spinning and turning white. I saw the figure of the Blessed Mother in the middle of the Sun. The most beautiful experience of my life. In July I invited Nancy to New Jersey and she accepted. While Nancy was here, the Blessed Mother appeared to her in my son Michael's room. Michael saw the Blessed Mother and while he was seeing her, I saw a golden glow around him. The glow went from shoulder to shoulder, it was something I had never seen before.

After my two pilgrimages to Conyers, and having Nancy here there was an urgency in my heart to return to Conyers as often as possible.

In August I had planned to go to Florida, instead, after much prayer, I went to Conyers and spent six glorious days there. When I first got there, I was greeted with the scent of roses. I was at the bus station. The last thing you smell there is roses!

After being in Conyers for a couple of days, I visited Nancy in her home. Nancy invited me into her Apparition Room for prayer along with Tom and Joanne Harris and Bob Spellman.

Shortly after we entered the room, I noticed a glow around

the statue of Our Loving Mother. I wouldn't dare say any-thing because I thought I was "just seeing things," making myself see what I wished to see.

As hard as I tried to keep up with the conversation in the room, I could not take my eyes off of the statue. The glow and the feeling of warmth was too strong. Nancy noticed my eyes fixed on the statue and without asking any questions, she said: "Yes, you see something by the statue and there is a presence there." Well! This was confirmation that I was not just seeing things. The question now was: Why me?

We started to pray and a few minutes later I saw a light glow around the crucifix on the wall; again, I thought I was seeing things, for me to see something twice in one night was just too much. Nancy said there was light around the crucifix. At this point I decided to say something about what I was seeing. I told Nancy that I did not see the light as she saw it but that I saw a light contouring the crucifix. Nancy asked me if I really saw that, and when I answered that I did, she confirmed that I was seeing the light as she saw it. My feet did not touch the ground for at least three days after this night. I am not worthy of such graces and I could not believe I had been blessed with such gifts.

I reluctantly left Conyers and returned to New Jersey. When I got home I prayed in front of the statue of Our Loving Mother that Michael has in his room where the Blessed Mother appeared to Nancy. As I was praying and giving thanks for all the graces I received in Conyers, the statue was glowing, suddenly her face changed to the face of Jesus. This had happened at Nancy's house while I was praying and I thought it was an optical illusion. Once more Nancy told me that I was having a vision not an optical illusion. I have been returning to Conyers every month since then, each month I receive more graces, more blessings, one of the best blessings of all is the friends I have made there and through Conyers. There is such love there, such feeling of Christianity, such peace. I thank God every day for the people I have met in, or through my association with, Conyers.

Having Nancy's friendship is a great grace for which I give thanks every day. Nancy turned out to be a sweet woman who does not put on airs, who accepted a cross along with the gift of seeing Jesus and his Mother, a friend to all who open their hearts to Jesus.

As I said before, I have been returning to Conyers every month since August and hope to one day live there, so that the Holy Hill is not so far as it is now even though I must admit, as long as it is in my heart, it's not far at all.

Oh! by the way, I now attend Mass daily whenever possible, no Sunday goes by without me attending Mass. I have been to confession often and my entire life has taken a turn I did not dream of a year ago. I have gone from being a short-tempered, impatient, impossible loud mouth to a more calm, more patient, more thoughtful loud mouth.

I must tell you that one of the many friends God gave me in Conyers is Joy Guillot. Joy and I would talk on the phone every time I called the farm. When I decided to go in August, Joy helped me find lodging and not only that but offered to put me up in her house. She picked me up at the station, and during my stay there, drove me everywhere. We had never met in person before, and, being from the New York Metropolitan area, to me this was not real. No one goes so far to help a stranger! Right? Wrong! There are beautiful, wonderful people, like Joy and her family, still around. I thank God every day for sending me Joy, Nancy, and the many friends He has sent me.

Testimony of Wilhelmina Kooymans

My name is Wilhelmina Kooymans. I now live in Duluth, Georgia.

My first experience was on August 23, 1988. It was the Feast of St. Rosa of Lima. I was invited by Nancy Fowler to pray the rosary at her home.

After we prayed the rosary, Nancy invited me into the room where Jesus appears to her. We knelt down before the Crucifix which hangs on the wall. As we started praying, I was thinking and praising the Lord for all the blessings he has bestowed on me. There was no sun shining into the room. Suddenly a bright Cross of Light appeared on the wall. The Cross of Light moved from one side of the Crucifix to the other side. Finally the light came to rest on the Crucifix. This lasted for ten minutes. A great peace and joy came over me. I believe this was a miracle.

Another Sunday afternoon, I was praying the rosary on the Holy Hill. I was asked to bear witness to a miracle in the sky. I saw an opening in the sky. In the opening I saw a round circle with the colors of a rainbow. Then I saw a white Cross bigger than the circle and over and above the circle. Inside the circle was a cross. After awhile the clouds covered the circle.

Many times I have smelled the fragrance of flowers and I have also seen The Blessed Mother kneeling in the sky. Those are such great blessings to me.

Testimony of Bill F. Erman

Dear Nancy Fowler and Our Loving Mother's children:
My wife (Rosemary) and I (Bill) visited the Farm at Conyers the Monday after Thanksgiving (November 30, 1992). We stopped there because our niece had related some most unusual things that she had experienced, and is still experiencing, as a result of her visits to Conyers. We were returning from a trip to visit our son's family in Florida and could only stay for about two hours before we continued on our way to Cincinnati. We arrived at the Farm a little before 10:00 a.m. It was a beautiful, sunny, peaceful day; no one else was around at the time; the store was not yet open; therefore, we visited the Apparition Room first. By the time we left the Apparition Room, the store had opened; we visited with one of the volunteers; we picked up several books; and I grabbed a rosary. (My wife had brought her rosary with her.) We walked to the Holy Hill and surveyed the scene: the altar, the crib set, the well, Nancy Fowler's home. I hate to admit it now, but, frankly, I really wasn't very impressed by anything I saw to this point. I asked my wife if she would like to say the rosary and she immediately agreed. We sat down in two of the chairs located around the Cross and began saying the rosary. (My wife chose the Glorious Mysteries.) I remember getting through the first two Hail Marys of the first decade, when suddenly I had a feeling of remarkable peace and the feeling that this was the most beautiful prayer in the world. Then, I actually felt something happen to my body (I have not been able to describe this feeling; I have never felt it before.) I then felt that I had no control over my emotions and I sobbed and sobbed uncontrollably. I kept repeating to Rosemary that I was overwhelmed, completely overwhelmed! Suddenly I had a most overwhelming feeling of love, total unconditional love for everyone—for God, for Rosemary, and *especially* for people with whom I was angry at the time and finally, it was as if God said everything will be all right, trust me. (I had been struggling with several problems that were totally consuming me and causing me misery prior to our visit to the Farm.) And then these feelings abruptly ended. The whole experience lasted about 5 minutes. I then said to my wife, "This truly is Holy Ground." In my 61 years on this earth, I have never experienced *anything* remotely like this. After some time in prayer and discussion, Rosemary and I walked hand-in-hand back to the farm; we passed three women, who were approaching the Holy Hill, but no one else. At first I didn't want to share this experience with anyone else; it was too personal, I was overwhelmed, and I didn't think anybody would believe me or really understand what I had experienced. In fact, I still have difficulty describing the strange feeling in my body that

preceded the love experience. I will say this: the feeling of love was *immense,* totally *unconditional,* and completely overwhelming!

I have been deeply affected by this experience, and I thank Jesus for this special gift.

> With deep love and prayers,
> Bill
> William F. Erman
> Cincinnati, OH
> January 24, 1993

Testimony of Joan Rathburn

Dear Nancy,

Thanks so much for sending the holy water to help me in my fight against cancer. I was so blessed to have many, many people offering prayers for me. God blessed me and my family with great peace during this trial. Each day I used the holy water and whether it was the holy water or the many prayers that were said or a combination of both—when they went in to remove part of my colon, they couldn't find cancer anywhere. Not even in my colon. God in His Mercy helped me through my pregnancy, blessed us with a healthy boy and got me through the operation with flying colors. We really believe a miracle has taken place even though because of my pregnancy there are no x-rays, etc. to prove it. I know in my heart that somehow God used my illness to bring people together and back to him. Who knows exactly what His plan was—I just know that many, many people are now giving Him praise and joy.

I continue to use the water every day and to bless both of my children!

Thanks ever so much.

> Joan Rathburn
> Trinity, North Carolina
> September 1992

Testimony of Helen Kent

Last December I wrote you about my granddaughter

Ashley Murray. She was there in January and was in the Apparition Room. It might also be of interest to know that Ashley was on the video—at the end. She is the small child (in a blue coat) that was being prayed over. My daughter Vickie, who was with her, stated that she thought Ashley may have seen something; for she kept telling her to "Look at the baby"—well, Ashley's health has greatly improved.

The story on Brian Terry—my grandson from Little Rock, Arkansas—is that in December he was diagnosed with anemia of eight hemoglobin—etiology unknown. They started him on iron and he had been on it one week when he came to Conyers and drank from the well in your yard. Two weeks later his checkup showed a jump to 14 in his hemoglobin—impossible for three weeks on nothing but iron. He has maintained this and is doing well.

On my September 13 visit (which was my 58th birthday) one of your volunteers prayed with me and she said the Lord wanted something special of me. Being used for this article was no plan of mine—it just happened—neither was the fact that so many of my children came with me. I just know Blessings are abundant.

Thank you Nancy for being the instrument you are and thank your husband and children for sacrificing much of their private life for our Mother's desire to reach her children.

I will pray for you and the grace to bear all. Jesus and Mary need you.

And please—if I can ever do anything—please I would love to help.

> Thank you and Bless you,
> Helen Kent
> Augusta, Georgia

Testimony of Mona Karam

My name is Mona Karam, born in Cairo, Egypt, and I immigrated to Canada as a teenager. I have a degree in accounting. I also speak and write in three different languages. I got married and moved to the U.S.A. I have two daughters and one granddaughter.

I read an article about Nancy Fowler. I got her phone number and called her. In July 1991, I went to Conyers with my sister from Canada and her husband and a group of other people. The minute I arrived at Nancy's home, I had the same feeling I had in Medjugorje. I bought two rosaries in Medjugorje for myself, one turned gold while I was in Medjugorje. The other did not. On August 13, 1991, I went to Nancy's to witness the apparition. I was praying the rosary when Mary, a friend of mine said, "Look at your rosary, it turned gold." That confirmed for me that both the apparitions in Medjugorje and at Conyers are authentic and not just a hoax.

We were praying the rosary in the Apparition Room with Nancy when Jesus told her "Mona, Mona, Mona," three times. "She is seeing the light." I said "Yes" because I was seeing the light around the cross and at times seeing what seemed like God the Father in light stretching his hand on top of the cross. The cross looked so different to me, like being suspended in the air in three dimension and after I saw the face of Jesus turning straight looking at me from the cross, tears were rolling down my cheeks. I was choking on my own tears and in my mind I was praising him, loving him and thanking our Holy Mother for bringing me so close to him at that time. This apparition is beyond description. I cannot put it in words to justify what I saw and how I felt.

I have had many experiences in Conyers, but I cannot put all of them in detail. On July 13, 1992 (my first anniversary going to Conyers) I saw the Blessed Mother materializing. She was glowing like the sun was behind her. I saw her lips moving, talking with Nancy, but I didn't hear her. She had the biggest smile when the crowd sang Ave Maria. I think that my gift from her was to see her.

On November 13, 1992, after the apparition, a group of us went to Nancy's house; we were in the dining room. Nancy was with George Collins in the Apparition Room. The doors were closed, but I could see the crucifix on the opposite wall in the room; there were no mirrors or glass to reflect the crucifix. Jesus looked alive and his head was not tilted; he was looking straight at me. In my mind, I asked him if what I was seeing was real. When the apparition was over, Carol Bradford was crying because she saw the same thing that I saw. Carol is Lutheran.

I have seen many pictures taken of the Blessed Mother and of Jesus and of saints whenever I go to Conyers. The biggest miracle to me is when I see the number of people going to Conyers rise from 50 to almost 48,000 people praying. To me that is the miracle. People are from every denomination, from all over the country and some from overseas. Most of the people go home with conversions in their hearts, and many return again and again.

I know that Nancy is called by God and that she is enduring the pressure bestowed upon her. That strength can only come from God, because no person like Nancy can endure without divine intervention.

Testimony of Kevin Boyar

Archbishop James P. Lyke
680 West Peach Tree Street, N.W.
Atlanta, Georgia 30308

Dear Archbishop Lyke:
Let me begin by professing my complete obedience to the church authority. Regardless of the issue, I adhere to the position taken by Rome.

The above having been said, I would like to relay to you my personal experiences in connection with the alleged apparitions of Conyers, Georgia.

I first heard of the events of Conyers in February of 1991. I proceeded to contact the visionary, Nancy Fowler, in an effort to learn more details about her claims and to ascertain her level of sincerity. I was sufficiently impressed with her humility and attitude of obedience that I booked a flight to come down (I live on Cape Cod, in Massachusetts) to investigate the situation first hand.

Prior to my departure, I again spoke with Nancy to work out the details of our meeting. During this subsequent conversation she more descriptively discussed her visions which included reference to "angels filling the sky, etc., etc." "Oh," I remember thinking to myself. "This lady sees angels too? What next, bigfoot?" Anyway, in spite of my newly rekindled skepticism (and perhaps more than anything else, due to my airline ticket obligation) I decided to see the trip through.

I arrived at Nancy's home on Saturday, February 23rd, at around 9 P.M., and we proceeded to talk for about two hours. One of my very first questions was why Jesus and Mary would possibly select her as an instrument. Nancy explained that Jesus had told her that He did not always choose the "best people" and that through her (because of her own faults and weaknesses) many would come to better understand His love and mercy. In addition, anyone who would spend any amount of time with Nancy would soon recognize that the sublime (in the very nature of their simplicity) yet profound (in their depth of truth) teachings that she would relay could not possibly come from her. "Not a bad response," I thought to myself, "but I'm not buying into this deal yet; not by a long shot."

The following afternoon, Sunday, February 24th, I attended the weekly prayer meeting, which at the time was taking place in Nancy's backyard. At around 3:15 P.M., the prayer of the rosary commenced with about 35 people in attendance. I knelt about nine feet away from Nancy.

After five minutes of group prayer, Nancy announced that the Blessed Mother was now among us. I didn't feel a thing. Suddenly, a woman to Nancy's immediate right exclaimed in an ecstatic voice, "the roses, the roses!" I inhaled deeply. . .nothing. A gentleman from the area approached me and suggested that I move closer to Nancy. I'd flown a thousand miles to get there so I decided that moving another few feet wasn't too much to ask (although I did mentally question why my positioning had anything to do with miracles).

Minutes later Nancy made another proclamation. "The sky is filled with angels. There's a magnificent angel right over there (pointing)." Others among the group began to gesture as well. Some sporadic, "yeh, yeh, I can see it," comments could be heard. I gazed in the direction of the extended fingers. "Is that what these guys are making all this fuss about?" I recall thinking. "I see the cloud that they're talking about. Sure, it's a little darker than the rest and maybe it does resemble the outline of an angel but, what the heck, I can see elephants up there too. If that's all there is to this Conyer's thing than this deal is pretty weak."

The "roses lady" again pronounced a floral presence but this time, however, her voice was echoed by a young man to Nancy's immediate left. I breathed in as fully as possible. . .and I smelled. . .wet dirt. Wet dirt. Mud! I hunched back somewhat dejectedly. "So," I thought to myself, "this is Conyers. Well, the least that I should do while I'm here is try and get in a prayerful rosary." At that very moment a puff of air passed over my face. Maybe a four inch by nine inch cylindrical breeze; something that I had never before experienced. And then it happened. . .the most magnificent scent I have ever experienced. . .the roses, the roses! I gasped out loud and fell back on my haunches. This was all true! I collapsed forward curling myself into a tight ball. I simply could not handle the magnitude of what was happening. I wanted to crawl into the earth and disappear. Tears poured down my face. For an instant, in confusion, my doubt resurfaced. This just could not be taking place. Again, the roses.

Archbishop, I apologize for what may sound like melodrama. There is simply no way for me to put into words the enormity of that moment. Mine was not merely a discovery of the truth of Conyers, mine was a confirmation of the Truth of God. A man, Jesus Christ, really did walk this earth two thousand years ago. He really did die for our salvation. He really was calling us back to Him. God is alive! (I know that this admission clearly illustrates the weakness of my previous faith. Be that as it may, the events of Conyers have brought me into a more intimate relationship with Christ than what I ever would have imagined could be.)

Then, in the midst of the miracle, it occurred to me. Here

I was in the middle of the Sorrowful Mysteries and I'm beaming with delight. How unworthy could I be? I had literally been given a gift from Heaven and was offering sacrilege for repayment. Then, just as suddenly, I recalled the words of Christ that had been read to me the previous evening: "See My love first, then see My suffering. If you see My suffering first and not My love, then you have missed My reason for coming. Tell men of My love. Show men My love, be My love in this world."

Archbishop, I have come to realize, through the events of Conyers, the real love of Jesus. I guess I always kind of imagined God as being stationed somewhere north west of the planet Pluto. Never contemplating for a moment that He really was right here. . .for me, and for you, and for everyone else. Please don't misinterpret my comments. I recognize full well that you have great faith without the need for any miraculous intervention. That's wonderful. Unfortunately, I'm one of the weak ones. Conyers has brought my faith into focus. At the conclusion of the prayer meeting, I remember running up to Nancy and throwing my arms around her. "Thank you so much," I said to her, "you've saved my life." "Not me," she responded, "thank Jesus."

Conyers has, and continues to be, of tremendous spiritual benefit. The witnessing of miracles can never be greater than receiving Our Lord in the Eucharist but, contrary to common apparition criticism, Conyers has helped to solidify this reality. The events in Georgia don't overshadow the Mass, nor do they purport or attempt to. Conyers reaffirms the glory of the Mass.

I know that to stay close to My Savior means frequent reception of the sacraments. In order to listen to Jesus, I must pray. Although He is always with me, I am not always with Him. As Jesus once told Nancy, *"Do you think that prayer brings Me to you?. . .Prayer brings you to Me."*

Archbishop, I absolutely cherish the divine kisses that I have received through the events in Conyers, Georgia. I realize, however, that my faith can never be based upon mystical experiences. If, for some unforseen reason, Conyers was ever "taken away from me" the absence could neither erase my personal experiences, nor negate my newly found intimate relationship with God. I realize that the church must move cautiously with respect to alleged apparitions for a myriad of reasons; all of which I accept and understand. I pray, however, that others will have the same opportunity to bring their faith to life that was given to me. Remember, there's a lot of us weak ones out there who need that hit on the head.

In the final analysis, one must look to the fruits of any alleged apparition to discern its value. Tremendous spiritual (and some physical) healings continue to take place along

99

with wonderful stories of conversion. I can personally attest to friends, and friends of friends, coming back to the church as a specific result of my testimony. I state this with humility. I know that I am nothing more than a witness. My witness, however, has been a catalyst for conversion. I know first hand of individuals going to confession for the first time in 15, 20, and 27 years! One particular man that I've spoken to is presently preparing a speech for his congregation that will be delivered in a couple of weeks pertaining to Our Blessed Virgin Mary; the church: Presbyterian!

I know that there has been some negative press recently about Nancy Fowler but condemnation by the media is nothing new. When Jesus tells Nancy that her body is a temple and that she should take better care of herself it is an example of divine intimacy. When the headlines sarcastically announce that GOD TELLS SELF-PROCLAIMED PROPHET TO GO ON A DIET, it is distortion that completely misses the point.

Nancy Fowler has been called to bear witness to the Living Presence of Jesus Christ. To do so she has been exposed to ridicule while simultaneously losing much of her personal life and most of her privacy. She in no way "profits" from the apparitions. However, Conyers isn't about Nancy Fowler. It's about God's Love and Mercy.

The teachings and messages stemming from Conyers are absolutely in alignment with the doctrine of the church. Thousands are coming together in prayer. The desire to seek out the reality of God for so many heretofore apathetic Catholics is, in itself, a miracle worthy of serious investigation.

There's nothing noticeably special about Nancy Fowler but that's just it. God has always chosen the little ones, Himself taking flesh as the son of a common carpenter.

Archbishop, please forgive me for my rambling but Conyers is very important to me. More to the point, Conyers can make a difference to an awful lot of people around this nation, and the world. I pray that your heart will remain open to the limitless ways in which God may choose to gather his children.

I am completely at your service should you, or your staff, choose to discuss this, or any other matter with me.

> In Christ,
> Kevin M. Boyar
> Cotuit, Massachusetts
> May 3, 1992

Testimony of Judith Singer

During the first week of June 1992 I was sent by my employer to Atlanta, GA, to take a work-related course of study. My husband, Wayne, accompanied me as he had research to do in that city. During the break from my studies, I was praying for my daughter-in-law who lives in Nevada and who had been hospitalized the previous day. A lady named Barbara, who sat next to me in the class, saw me praying and asked whether I was Catholic. I replied I was, and she prayed with me. Then she told me about Conyers, GA where Jesus and the Blessed Mother had appeared. Barbara asked me if I would like to drive to Conyers with her and two other women taking the course; and I replied that I would, and that I was sure my husband would be happy to drive us there.

After class on the event of June 3rd, we proceeded to drive to Conyers, located approximately 30 miles east of Atlanta. During the drive, Barbara told us that the apparition took place at the home of Nancy Fowler and that she had spoken with Nancy who assured her that we were welcome on the property at any time, and that even if she could not personally join us, we were to feel free to take holy water from the well at the site of the shrine.

It was becoming dark as we arrived in Conyers, and the road led us through sparsely populated farmland. After attempting unsuccessfully to find the Fowler house, we were directed by a man and woman working a field to a nearby farmhouse. There was no one home, but we followed the signs for "Pilgrim Parking" and found ourselves at a house behind which was a large field with the Stations of the Cross around the perimeter, and a shrine built in the middle.

The farm was very beautiful and peaceful. As the group went ahead I walked onto the porch of a side room that extended from the main house; and I peeked into what I was later to learn was called the Apparition Room. There were some photographs tacked to the front door of the Apparition Room, but by now it was too dark to see clearly what the photographs showed.

Then, as I walked on to rejoin the group, I smelled candles and incense. I prayed and took four stones from the path leading to the altar to Jesus and Mary in the middle of the field behind the house. I had also prayed at another shrine to the Blessed Mother in the yard close to the house. During our inspection of the field and the area closer to the house we were unable to find the well and were disappointed as we had all wanted to take some Holy Water back with us.

Next to the house itself was a small building that was closed, but signs outside indicated that books about Jesus and the Blessed Mother and the Conyers story were given out there.

The next day during a break from our classwork, a young man named Luis said he was going to Conyers. We told him to go early, and that we had not found the well. The following day Luis advised us that while there had indeed been apparitions at the location we visited, known simply as "The Farm," the well was located on Nancy Fowler's property and that was a short distance away. That is where the initial apparition took place. (Interestingly, as we were returning to Atlanta that first night we passed a reflective road marker in the form of a crucifix and my husband said that must be the place, but we all giggled that it couldn't have been so obvious.)

After hearing Luis restate how hospitable Nancy was, and how she welcomes visitors I realized that not only did I want to go back to Conyers to visit the shrine, I actually felt compelled to.

By now it was Friday, June 5th. I invited Barbara to accompany me after class, but she had a late afternoon flight to catch. She did tell me, however, that she expected to return to Conyers on June 13th with a group of fellow-Floridians who were making a pilgrimage. It was expected that 20,000 people in total would visit Conyers that day.

When Wayne met me for lunch, I asked him to drive me back that afternoon and he said he would be glad to. This time, armed with exact directions, we found Nancy Fowler's house with ease. The well was near the house, quite close to where we parked our car; and the first thing we did was fill two bottles we had brought with us with Holy Water. The well was activated by manipulating an old-fashioned hand pump.

Sitting by the well were a woman of my age, a young girl in her late teens and a young man of the same age named Michael. Michael told us it was alright to drink the water from the well—he did so every day. He explained that he comes to the shrine almost every day to help Nancy in any way he can, and to videotape what happens at the site. He said that he had often seen angels and smelled roses at the shrine. We drank some of the water, which tasted cool and fresh, and then walked to the shrine located in the field behind the Fowler house. The shrine was made of large field stones, mortared together, in the shape of a cross approximately ten feet long. This cross rested flat on the ground, and at the head of this stone cross stood a wooden cross of approximately life-size.

At the shrine we met a lovely young woman named Margaret Shea who, along with her mother and the young girl we had met at the well, had come to Conyers on a pilgrimage. Margaret told us that Nancy had been asked by the Lord to buy the property on which we now stood, and to build the shrine as it exists. Furthermore, she was ordered to search the entire property to find the wood that comprises the crucifix at the head of the shrine. She was told that the wood was already prepared, and she would know it when she saw it. In fact, the wood she found was finished as heavy, squared-off timbers; and the cross piece contained heavy bolts in the position one would expect to secure extended arms.

Margaret pointed to a mark on the back of the wooden cross's upright which she identified as an outline of Mary. She said that Nancy Fowler, not originally recognizing the significance of the mark, had tried to scrub it out; but her priest had told her not to. I was unable to see Mary in the mark; but instead I saw very clearly a profile of Our Lady of Fatima with her beautiful crown. When I pointed this out all the others saw it clearly too.

At the middle of the stone shrine was a small statue of Jesus and at the foot of the shrine was a small statue of the Blessed Mother. Visitors have left prayer beads on the shrine and the statue of the Blessed Mother was draped with a silver rosary.

Now, this is the part I was brought here to tell. As we were standing together around the shrine, Michael said he smelled something. He said it smelled like roses and he asked me if I was wearing perfume. I said that I had put on a little at 8:00 A.M., but none since then. He asked if any of us [me, Wayne, Margaret, her mother, and a young man in his late teens] smelled anything. I answered "No" and no one else said anything. Michael then called our attention to the birds in the trees bordering the field. They appeared agitated and were chirping loudly. Michael said, "Do you hear the birds chirping? When they chirp so loudly it means the Blessed Mother will appear." I remember thinking "We're in the country—of course the birds are going to chirp!" Michael went on to say he was now smelling cinnamon. I mentioned that I had smelled incense that evening when we visited the farm.

Then Michael pointed to the sky and said "Look at the cross in the clouds! See, there's a little one. . .and see, look at the big one" I looked but I didn't see the crosses. Then the sun went behind an enormous bank of clouds. The rays from the sun, along with what looked like heavy shadows, shined up and out from the tops of the clouds; and many shined horizontally, but none of the rays shined down towards the earth as I would have expected them to do. In the center of the rays, on top of the clouds, was an opening that looked as if the top of a head—or hair—was in the middle. Michael saw this too and said "Look. Doesn't there seem to be something in the center of it?" Then one soft, single ray shined down. As we all looked up, the sun reappeared from the large cloud bank. I guarded my eyes as I looked up and suddenly I saw the sun dance in the sky. I heard Michael say "See, it's dancing." I could not take my eyes away. All I could say was "I see it." Then the sun started to spin in the sky. Michael said, "Look. Now it's spinning." I said excitedly, "Yes, yes, I see it." This activity lasted about fifteen seconds.

I turned to look at my husband who was standing about ten feet away on a slight rise of the hill. On his left thigh, just above where his left leg had been amputated, was a large gold mark. I looked at the rest of him thinking that the sun had affected my vision; but the only place the gold mark appeared was on his thigh. His trousers were white and his shirt was blue. There were little sparkles, like he was dusted with glitter on his shirt; but the mark on his leg was what captured my attention.

No one said a word at this time. Some distance away, next to Nancy Fowler's house, I saw a little boy standing by a fence. He was totally gold. I turned to the shrine and the Blessed Mother was gold. Everything in the area to the front, back and sides of her was gold, including her rosary and the rosaries that had been left on the shrine. The shrine was surrounded by small white decorative stones interspersed with larger paving stones on which supplicants kneel. These paving stones appeared normal, but the decorative stones were gold.

The young woman, Margaret, had a gold mark on her leg. I inspected my clothing to see whether I had any gold on me. I looked at the sleeves of my white jacket and at my slacks and saw nothing. Then I turned my hands over and my palms were all gold. At this point, Margaret's mother said, "Look at the stones." She pointed to what I had observed. Then she pointed to the same spot on Margaret's leg that I had seen. I said, "Look at the Blessed Mother" and she saw the Blessed Mother in gold as I did and saw the Holy Rosary in gold.

Margaret asked us to pray the Holy Rosary with her. She said that is what the Blessed Mother wants us to do when she appears. I have never said the Holy Rosary but of course I agreed and we followed as she led us in prayer. When we finished she turned and thanked me. She said she wanted to give me a gift, and she hugged me and gave me a special blessing. I turned to my husband, hugged him, and passed the gift on to him.

We stayed a while and other people joined us including the little boy I had seen as all gold earlier. He was dressed all in blue denim and what had appeared as a gold ball was the jacket he was carrying rolled up. The only gold on him now was his golden hair. Various people spoke about what had brought them to Conyers; however, neither Margaret's mother nor I discussed what we had seen. It was too humbling an experience and was too fresh in our minds.

Michael, on the other hand, was elated that he had seen the sun dance and said that he hoped the videotape he had taken would come out well. He then videotaped all of us at the shrine and said that people all over the world would see us.

When we left the shrine, I asked Wayne to take me back to the farm we had gone to on our original visit. This time the book office was open. Inside, I met Luis—my classmate—and told him what had happened at Nancy's. Needless to say I had cried after my experience and was still rather emotional; but later my husband told me that I had been crying all during the time when I saw the sun dance and spin, as well as during the visitation.

The volunteers who give out the books at the farmhouse listened to my story and said it had been a Blessing. They also said that on occasion they had heard about seeing gold as a sign of the Blessed Mother's presence. While at the farm I went to the Apparition Room and prayed and thanked Jesus for giving me this wonderful Blessing. I saw baskets filled with petitions and I was grateful that I could personally pray for my family knowing that Jesus knew what was in my heart. I especially wanted to thank Jesus and the Blessed Mother for the revelation I had witnessed. Then I went back to the book room because even though the sign said "One Book Per Family" my husband told me to ask for one for my sister. The lady there said she thought the Blessed Mother would say "yes" and she gave me the other book. As I was leaving, she walked out with me.

Tacked to the side of the building were the photographs that had originally been attached to the door of the Apparition Room, and that I had been unable to see in the dark when we first visited the farm. What I saw in the photos was what I had just witnessed at the shrine. The clouds and the rays were just as I had seen them not an hour earlier. Underneath the clouds was what I took to be the statue of the Blessed Mother, bathed in gold, as I had seen her. I asked if someone had taken a picture of the Blessed Mother's statue at the shrine when the clouds were that way. The lady said that was not a picture of the statue at all. Rather, that was what developed on the film when someone had taken a picture of the clouds. In other words, the gold Blessed Mother was what had appeared in the sky under the clouds.

I kept saying, "But that is the Blessed Mother at the shrine." She said, "No. It is the visitation—the apparition— that appeared on the film." I almost did not understand. Then I told her that was exactly what I had seen at the shrine; and all the while I was surrounded by a feeling of peace, joy and stillness. Now I knew beyond any doubt that the Blessed Mother had been all around us at the shrine.

The next day at breakfast I asked Wayne to tell me his impressions. He said it was very spiritual, and that Margaret's mother and I had indeed pointed to the same places when describing to each other where we saw gold. He told me that I was crying when I looked around and saw the gold. I asked him why, when I turned to look at him after seeing the sun dance and spin, he was up on that little hill some distance from me. He replied that he was standing next to me the whole time—within arm's length. I don't remember anyone being around me after I saw the sun's actions. The only thing I remember being close to was the shrine and the cross leading to Our Lady in gold—Our Loving Mother.

When I had originally gone into the book room at the farm, I had been wondering what all this meant. What did God want me to do? Why did He give me this Blessing? As I was thinking this very thought, my husband handed me the book that is given to each family that visits Conyers. On the book's cover are the words "What do you ask of me?" "TO BEAR WITNESS THAT I AM THE LIVING SON OF GOD."

Ms. Judith Singer
Tampa, Florida

Testimony of Lisa Weaver

My name is Lisa Weaver. I am 35 years old. I've been married to the same man for 15 years and we are very happy together. It has been easy for us to stay together because we not only love each other, but we are also best friends. After seven years of marriage we adopted our first child, and 2½ years later our second. I also have a *very* close relationship with my parents, brother and sister and their families. We are *often* together as a family, not just on special occasions.

Anyway, I am going along, day after day, living in my own little safe world thinking everything is great. Knowing all along something isn't right. Something's missing. The sad part is that I knew it was Jesus Christ, but was not willing to totally give myself to Him. Totally trust Him. I also knew I should be in church and should be raising my children in church, but *no way!* It's much too hard to get out of bed. I'm tired. I *deserve* my rest.

Until Conyers! I was there December 13, 1992, and I can't begin to tell you how it affected me. All I want to do is love my Lord and Blessed Mother more and more and spread His words. I pray for the Holy Spirit to lead me and allow God's Love to shine through me for His Glory.

Thank you for allowing me to share this with you, and please remember me in your prayers.

In Christ's Love,
Lisa Weaver

106

Shreveport, Louisiana

P.S. I'll be back for the February 13th and March 13th apparitions.

Testimony of Rick Green

[Rick Green is thirty-five years old and lives in Conyers, Georgia. He works twelve-hour shifts at a local industrial plant. In May 1992 Rick's wife heard about Conyers and visited there. She brought the book To Bear Witness That I am the Living Son of God back to her home and Rick read it, went to Conyers and experienced a spiritual conversion of his heart as did his wife.]

December 24, 1992, my wife, my handicapped daughter, Amanda, and I decided to go to the Holy Hill in Conyers. My wife wanted a picture of the miracle of the sun. She said, "The sun is spinning like crazy." We took a picture and didn't think we got anything. I was looking at the pictures she took and one clearly has wings in it and the other has a cross in it. We had gone to see a new statue that day at Conyers. [The Statue of Our Lady of Fatima was delivered December 12th in Conyers.] My wife and I took a few pictures. I smelled something sweet, and thought maybe it was someone's perfume. I found out later that other people smelled it too. We looked at our pictures, and they were blurry. I was going to throw them away and one caught my eye; there was a "realness" about it. I called my wife over and she thought so too.

We went home and went to Christmas Eve vigil. There was a great peace with us this year. On Christmas, we wanted to go back to the Holy Hill. I wanted to see the beautiful statue again. I took a picture and stuck it in my pocket. As I was about to take another picture, I noted that under the left cheekbone in the first picture of the Blessed Mother, there appeared to be a pink color. I took another picture and then another. I noticed a blur in front of my eyes as I looked into the face of Our Lady. It seemed as if light was really radiating. Then I looked and realized the Lady was looking at me. I told my wife that she was there! I had a great feeling of love bursting inside me. I didn't know what to do. She was smiling at me. It was so real. The light kept getting brighter. Her face was in living color and there was light all around her nose and mouth. I left feeling that God had given me a great gift. I was sure I had seen the Blessed Mother. I will never forget the experience as long as I live.

When I showed the pictures I had taken at my place of work, this fella asked me if I had moved before I took the second picture. I said, "No." He said, "Her head has changed positions."

[Rick's pictures are included in the text. It is significant to note that the Statue of Mary that he refers to is solid white, with no distinguishable features. Rich and his wife received spiritual conversions.]

Testimony of Jack Labarga

I was born into the Catholic Faith. My parents had me baptized, communed, and confirmed in the Catholic Church. I never really cared much for church since I never liked having to obey or follow orders.

After confirmation, I left the church knowing that I was never to return. God never existed and therefore God could never equal love.

I was surrounded by a lot of love from my parents but not having understood what love was I could not either appreciate or give any of it back. I also learned the art of using and manipulating all those around me, since my idea of a relation was simply based on temporary feelings and nothing very deep.

Having grown up without any real direction I began to set up my own rules without regards for anyone else's feelings but my own.

My relationship with my parents and all my loved ones gave them a lot of pain as I was a 24-hour display of self-will running riot.

Instant pleasure and money became my God. Material possessions and showing off what I was attaining was what this life was all about.

One day the insanity finally got to my wife and children and I became persona non grata at our house (for sure not a home). My wife was seeking a divorce and an injunction to keep me away from the house.

She suggested that I needed to get into a 12-step program if I wanted to be any kind of father to my children. Having been the manipulator that I had become, I decided that I would get into a 12-step program to please my wife. I thought she would soon feel pity, come to my rescue with children in tow and I could go on living my same old life.

However, the opposite happened. She kept her distance from me and kept working on the divorce. I, on the other hand, now felt emotionally bankrupt and financially bankrupt as well.

Now as I look back, that was really the beginning of God's work in my life. I was now losing everything material but more important I was losing my loved ones (my first encounter with love).

At this time someone suggested that I go see Pastor Conny, at a place called St. Francis. The mission of St. Francis is a place where people like me go to get their lives in order and hopefully turn life around enough to make a contribution to our society.

I agreed to see Pastor Conny because I did not have a place to go and I was scared. I was now seeing life without the help of alcohol and frankly I was not emotionally fit to handle reality.

After I met with Pastor Conny and agreed to come live there I realized that there was more to this place than met the eye. This place had a chapel. From the first night, I started coming into the chapel and accused God for all my problems. I was an inferno of hate and anger. I felt the only reason this was happening was because God was full of hate and I would never, ever trust this hateful force with my life and that of my wife and my children.

After about 90 days at St. Francis, I decided that suicide was the only answer. I took myself out for a day drive. I wanted to find the perfect spot to end my life, since I did not want my children to find my body. At this point, I felt guilt, loneliness, despair, and fear like never before. I cried for hours: just me, the suicide site, and my fears. I got so scared that I rushed back to St. Francis. Upon my return, Pastor asked me to come into his office and asked me how my day had been. Once more I started to cry with fear. I had no direction and the prospects seemed remote.

Pastor Conny, who is a master at what he does, asked me if I was open to enter into a non-binding contract with God. He used the term contract because he knew that I could relate to contracts and especially non-binding ones. I agreed to give God a try since I was too scared to end my life and therefore my choices were pretty limited.

Pastor took me into the same chapel I used to pace up and down the aisle cursing God and asked me to kneel at the altar. All I could do was cry while he kept his hand on my head in prayer. Suddenly I felt for the first time a calmness and warmth I had not felt before, or if I had, I did not know it.

I was asked that if I wanted to keep that feeling, I had to agree to start the morning on my knees and end the day the same.

Within the next several months my wife dropped the

divorce. I was still living at St. Francis; however, I was dating my wife and the children were becoming increasingly important in my life.

My career was on the up and up and once again I found the ability to start attaining material things and recognition from others as my travels would take me all over the world. This was 1983. I was 32 years old and I was back and this time I not only had a clear head but I had my best weapon, prayer and God.

From 1983 until 1990 I was doing exactly everything I wanted. I was all over the world meeting with the extremely wealthy and some of the most powerful leaders in the world. Going on missions that involved decisions affecting relationships between nations.

All of a sudden, there I am in Tokyo, Japan, in November 1990 for the coronation of Emperor Hirohito. The Chairman of our company was hosting a dinner for several heads of state and as I sat there I began to realize that I was again on a path to a gross misuse of the gifts that had been granted me.

I had my family back, but I was never around. Thanks to God, I had regained all that I had lost and gained a lot more. It hit me that I had taken advantage of the gifts that God had given me and selfishly kept it all to myself. I was a thief of God's grace and never looked to see how I could give some of it back. I was not on a spiritual journey with God, but at the edge of turning my soul over to the dark side as payment for financial rewards.

Once more I sat with Pastor Conny; he helped me to take a good look at my situation and we jointly wrote my letter of resignation.

Now, as a consultant and with less money, I began spending more time with my wife and children, more time at St. Francis, and more time searching for spirituality.

For about 3 years I had been talking about going to Medjugorje, Yugoslavia; however, I was really enjoying the lack of traveling and never made a strong effort.

Once again Pastor Conny directs me: he gave me a copy of *Queen of the Cosmos*. For the first time, I was beginning to feel something I never felt before. A closeness with the Virgin Mary and a hunger to know Her. I began to read more about the Blessed Mother and what my relationship to Her is all about. In February 1993 my mother-in-law comes to visit and tells me that she had heard that the Blessed Mother may be appearing to a woman in Georgia.

I again went to Pastor Conny and told him that I felt that my attention had been on too many things of this world and that I needed to focus on the Blessed Mother and furthermore that I had heard in my head to head up Highway 75 (from Florida) to Conyers. He answered quickly, "Let's call, find out the details, and make the arrangements; we are both going."

Within 3 weeks, Pastor Conny, my wife Karen, Steve, Cathy, Linda, and I were headed for Conyers to be present at the March 13, 1993, apparition.

March 13, 1993, we woke up to "the storm of the century." We had come too far to turn back. When we arrived at the farm the ground was already covered with snow. It was impressive to see so many people, many without the proper clothing, going up and down the hills helping one another. Many were walking in small prayer groups saying the Rosary and all seemed to be there out of love for Mary and Jesus.

Our first stop was at the well to get our jugs full of Holy Water. I spilled the water all over my arms and was stunned that the water was warming me instead of (under normal circumstances) making me cold. I called out to Pastor, Karen, anybody that could hear me, "The water is warm! The water is warm!" Then, as others validated my finding, another supernatural happening. In the middle of the storm, winds blowing, snow at blizzard-type condition, we were hit with wonderful smell of roses. Again, we were stunned but also now feeling grateful and humble.

As we walked around the farm now the police were asking folks to head back as the roads were closing. We decided to pile into my car for warmth and to say the Rosary. All of a sudden, six people piled into my snow-covered car as we prayed the Rosary. Shortly thereafter, we were told to leave by police order. We left; however, I knew that I would be back.

Driving back, I knew that I was coming from a very special place. One that has to this day completely changed my life.

After the first trip (3-13-93), my Rosary and prayer time became my most important part of the day. Fasting on Wednesday and Friday a part of my life and my hunger for Jesus, Mary, and Joseph a full-time hunger.

April 13, 1993, back to Conyers. I arranged my schedule so that nothing would interfere with my meeting with Mary. Pastor and Karen (my wife) could not make it. However, Steve and Cathy did; also this time we had five other friends that wanted a piece of what we had received. I should mention that one of the five had, during the Reagan and later the Bush days, served on a Presidential Commission. His ten years had ended with his resignation due to differences with the congress.

On April 13, 1993, I did not smell roses. However, my experience was more inside of me. As on apparition day the crowds begin to pray the Rosary and other prayers at approximately 12:00 noon.

All of a sudden I began to experience incredible heart beats and I thought I was having a heart attack. I told our group that I had to leave and would return later. I had not walked 20 steps when the announcement was made that the Blessed Mother had arrived. Instantly my heart returned to normal and as I stood there and looked at the crowd I felt not only peace but a sense of love and forgiveness towards others that was so awesome I could do nothing but cry. I felt her presence and I felt her love; I felt comfortably helpless knowing the power of Jesus.

I returned even more hungry than before and also much more emotional. I spent many hours with Pastor Conny as he helped me to receive and understand our Mother's blessings. I have shed many tears of joy out of love for her. I found myself one evening in Washington D.C. going back to my hotel in the middle of a reception so that I could read books about Mary. In the hotel room reading about Mary, I realized that my love was so strong that nothing in this world matters to me as my eternal relation with Mary, Jesus, Joseph, the Angels, and the Saints.

I had made a decision not to go back to Conyers for the May 13 apparition. However, our Loving Mother had other plans. I sat (as now a regular habit in the mornings) praying my Rosary, when all of a sudden I heard a clear request. "You are going back to Conyers." I stopped praying and I said, "Mother Mary, you have asked me to pray the Rosary every day and I do. You have asked me to fast every Wednesday and Friday and I do. Please don't ask me to keep going back and forth cause I just can't do it. Our Loving Mother, let me finish my prayers." I sat at my desk ready to organize my day; I picked up my pen and my pad and I wrote, "Don't quit now, we just began." I called Pastor and told him what had happened and we both agreed. I was going back to Conyers.

May 10, back to Conyers, not only for the apparition but for a very special meeting with Nancy Fowler and 3 days of wonderful prayer time. Pastor Conny, John, and Kerry joined us. It was on this trip that I felt for the first time the real meaning of the peace of God that passes all understanding. Then on the 13th, Mary treated us to an incredible display of her presence amongst us.

I have always been searching to be with winners and I have been looking in all the wrong places. I have finally found the crown I have been looking for, they are all around Jesus, Mary, and Joseph.

Thank you, Mother Mary, Queen of Peace, for leading me to eternal life. I have found Shangrila.

> Jack Labarga
> Washington, DC
> May 18, 1993

P.S. The friend that resigned his post in Washington

because of Congress received a letter one day after his return from Conyers, whereby the Congress of the United States was recognizing him for his efforts and wished for him to leave for Puerto Rico and co-chair a conference on behalf of the commission from which he had had to resign.

P.P.S. Cathy gave up smoking immediately after her first return from Conyers.

Jesus: *Bring the new ones, the old ones, the lost ones, the rebellious ones, the smart ones, the proud ones, the lame ones; bring them all for I am the one who heals.*

To Nancy Fowler
of Conyers, Georgia

Letter from Mary Bernoit

Dear Nancy,
Please accept these maple candies which we send to you again. This time at Easter time. We hope you and your family enjoy them.

Thank you for sending me those medals blessed by Our Blessed Mother. I will continue to distribute them.

Lent has been a very important season for our family spiritually. With God's grace we have grown closer to Him.

We continue to hold a family prayer night in our church each week (as requested by Our Lady in Green Bay, Wisconsin). Attendance is very low; besides our family of six, there are five to seven older people over the age of sixty. Young families just don't seem to be interested and even the older folks are not coming in great numbers. I think everyone has forgotten the importance and value of prayer. No wonder Jesus is sad.

We would like to come to visit your Holy Hill again and maybe even be present for Our Lady's apparition (if we could be there on the 13th of the month). I have distributed God's healing water to several people. I know of two cures. One, a little girl (given the Conyers water in a bottle) was healed of scoliosis, documented by an x-ray. The second healing—I was recently healed of a problem with my cervix which caused abnormal pap smears for several years. Praise be Jesus! Are you gathering documentation on healings? Anyway, we will visit you when we can. It's a long trip from New Hampshire!

We send you our best wishes for a Holy and Joyous Easter. We keep you in our prayers, Nancy.
May God's Love and Pace fill you at Easter and always. In the names of Jesus and Mary,

Mary Bernoit
Hanover, NH

Letter from Alicia Medina

July 10, 1992

Bishop Lyke
Atlanta, Georgia

Dear Bishop Lyke:
I am taking this opportunity to write to you and wish you speedy recovery. Many persons including myself are praying for your health. I would also like to tell you a little about the wonderful blessings I have received this past year. I truly believe my life has changed since the first time I heard about the apparitions in a small town called Conyers, Georgia. In January 1991 my father was diagnosed with Cancer in the lung, throat and skull. This came as a big surprise to my family as my father only went to get a check-up due to a cold. I later took my father to various doctors and they all agreed with what we had first been told. Bishop Lyke, my father was 79 years old, but I was not ready to let him go. The doctors told me he had very little time and there was nothing that could be done. I spoke to God and asked Him if it would be possible to let my father stay with us for a while longer. If he was going to suffer very much, I asked God to take him away in his sleep with no pain. As the month went by my father got worse—he couldn't go out and walk anymore. He was already using oxygen, he also had a fever that would not go away, and the doctors informed me that he had that fever because of the cancer in his lung and that fever will not go away. I was so sad to see my mother and father suffer so much. Bishop Lyke, I prayed a lot, but never went to church or prayed the rosary or felt inner peace. With everything that was going on, I took a fall and broke a disc in three places. I began to get very, very depressed. One day a very close friend from Miami received the messages from Our Loving Mother at Conyers, Georgia. She told me about it, but I did not pay much attention. My friend decided to go to Conyers and asked me to go, but I just couldn't because of the pain in my

back and legs. So she went and she came back such a different person, she went back to church, she started to learn the rosary and pray the rosary every day. She always was a very, very special person, but after the blessings she received at Conyers, she is closer to God than ever. She brought Holy Water from the Holy Hill at Nancy Fowler's home and gave it to me with so much love. At that time I gave the Holy Water to my parents; I drank the Holy Water and put a Miraculous Medal in my father's wallet. I prayed to God for a Miracle and began to read Our Loving Mother's messages. My fried met Nancy Fowler and she was very taken by Mrs. Fowler. She was sure that Mrs. Fowler was an honest and beautiful person that through her Our Loving Mother was sending messages to the United States to bring people closer to God.

I went to the hospital on June 12, 1991, to undergo surgery. The doctors had told my husband it was a tough operation and I may have to go through therapy. I kept thinking about my father and my daughters and how much they needed me. Bishop Lyke, somehow after having the Holy Water and reading the messages, I went into surgery at peace and leaving everything in God's hands. I had experienced seeing Blessed Mother in the Sky and the Sacred Heart of Jesus, the day after my friend returned from Conyers. I knew that my life had to change and that I had to learn again to have faith. With all those blessings I made it through my back operation strong and with peace. After eight days I left the Hospital in heels and giving thanks to God and his Mother for such success in my operation. The doctors informed me I did not have to have any kind of therapy. My family could not believe it. It was truly a blessing. When I returned home, my father was not on oxygen; he told me not to worry about him anymore because he was going to be fine.

After about a month I asked my doctors if I could go to Conyers. I needed so much to go over to the Holy Hill and thank God and Our Loving Mother. The day finally came that I was able to go to Conyers. Bishop Lyke, I can't begin to express the wonderful feelings and blessing I received. I was also finally able to meet Nancy Fowler, that lady that I have heard so much about. After I met Nancy, I had proven to myself that she was saying the absolute truth and she is truly a wonderful and loving person. I knew that God had chosen her to communicate his words and his Blessed Mother's words to the United States. I feel so much peace when I go to Conyers to visit the Holy Hill and pray that I wish to return time after time. I have had so many experiences there together with my children. I do not deserve all the wonderful blessing God has given me. I have returned to the church, I go to mass on Sundays and also daily, if I can. I pray the rosary and I feel so much inner peace.

Bishop Lyke, two months ago I took my father to the

doctor who's been seeing him for the cancer, and he had a scan and x-rays done on him. The doctor told me there is no trace of cancer. The lung is clear and my father's fever has been gone since my operation. This is a true miracle of God. My father is an 80-year-old gentleman who had only a few months to stay on with his family, now he is completely well and living life to his fullest.

There is so much more I could share with you of my experiences in Conyers, Georgia.

Thank you so much for taking time to read my letter. I pray every day for Nancy Fowler, her family, and for many people to return to God through Our Loving Mother's messages.

May God Bless you and always keep you in his care,

Alicia M. Medina
Miami, Florida 33183

Letter from Brenda Branch

Archbishop James Lyke
680 West Peachtree St., N.W.
Atlanta, Georgia

Archbishop Lyke,
I am writing this letter because a friend of mine, Mr. Roger Haddad, has asked me to do so as a favor to him. He wanted me to share an experience I had recently had.

Let me start by introducing myself. My name is Brenda Branch and I am from Rocky Mount, N.C. I am a Christian, but not of the Catholic faith. I am a Baptist because is what I have chosen.

Mr. Haddad and myself work for the same company, only in different states. Roger was at our plant in January following some special samples which were being run. While Roger was here he told myself and some of my co-workers about a Mrs. Nancy Fowler he had met and about some of the wonderful things he had seen happening in Conyers, Georgia.

Before Roger left our plant on Thursday that week, I told him my daughter had been sick and was to have some surgery on Tuesday of the next week. I asked him if he could possibly send me some of the water from Conyers. I wanted my daughter to have this water before her surgery. Roger returned to South Carolina on Thursday, sent the water and

I received it on Friday.

Now, I tell you of my experience with the water, I must go back to Tuesday of that week. While dressing for work that morning, I accidentally scraped the edge of a mole located on my shoulder. The next few days this mole became quite sore; to the point that clothes rubbing it bothered me. By Thursday, a red circle had appeared beneath the mole and I noticed that night that the mole seemed to be turning a strange purple color. Friday, I debated as to whether I should see a doctor or not. I decided to wait the week-end and if it was not better on Monday, I would see my doctor. That day I received the blessed water from Roger. That night my shoulder was quite sore and even more red around the mole. Before going to bed that night I said a prayer and rubbed the water on the mole. The next morning when I awoke, I noticed my shoulder did not feel sore any more. I looked to see if the purplish color had gone from the mole. Not only had the redness (ALL) gone from the spot, but the entire mole had disappeared! There was absolutely nothing there any longer.

I cannot offer any explanations or medical reasons for what happened; I can only say that in my heart I believe it happened because of the water and my faith in God.

I related what had happened to Roger and he in turn asked me to share it with you. Let me say thank you for your time.

Sincerely,
Brenda B. Branch
Rocky Mount, N.C.

Letter from Virginia Asaro

Dear Nancy,

My Mom had cataract surgery; the Dr. was not pleased with the outcome so he put her down for Cornea transplant, her Cornea was shattered, the doctor said it will never heal and we needed a miracle. A friend of mine came to your Holy Ground with my petition for a Miracle for Mom's eye. She left on Tuesday, Mom's appointment was Thursday, back to the doctor of Jewish Faith; he could not believe it, the Cornea was, as the doctor said, healed, except for one tiny spot. His exact words were, "This is unbelievable. A cornea like your Mom has, no way can heal by itself." So we are thanking Jesus for a beautiful Xmas. And we are rejoicing.

Virginia Asaro
Gloucester, MA
February, 1991

Testimony of Margaret Laurent:

In June, 1992, I was diagnosed as having a malignant melanoma on the retina of my left eye. This is a very rare form of cancer and at one time it meant immediate removal of the eye in order to save the patient's life. I was offered two options, removal of the eye or an attempt to save the eye and kill the cancer cells by implanting a radium plaque over the site of the tumor for a particular length of time, in my case it would be one week. I felt I should try the radium treatment and my doctor, Dr. Barrett Haik, agreed that I was a good candidate for the plaque.

I entered the hospital that July and the radium plaque was surgically implanted onto the eyeball. After a week the plaque was surgically removed and I returned home. Several office visits to the doctor were required and each visit showed the tumor was shrinking more rapidly than ever expected. Both Dr. Haik and his associate, Dr. Ainbinder who was also deeply involved in my treatment, said they had never seen a tumor react this way and termed it miraculous. I had been told from the beginning it would be a year before the doctors could tell if the cancer cells had been killed.

In early October, my husband and I and some other family members took a vacation trip to Tennessee. While there I told my husband I thought I would like to go to Conyers on the way home and he agreed. The rest of the family returned to Louisiana and we went on to Conyers. I had been doubtful as to whether or not to go to Georgia and kept debating with myself about it. I finally said, "Mary, please tell me what to do, should we go home or go to Conyers?" I distinctly heard her say, "Come." All doubt was removed and we went to Conyers knowing nothing about the place except that a woman named Nancy was receiving Apparitions from the Blessed Mother on the 13th of each month. It took some doing but we finally found Nancy's home and the farm. As I walked on the Holy Hill (I didn't know at the time it was called the Holy Hill) I experienced a sense of Presence and of Power I could not explain. My knees felt weak and my face felt numb. I was completely overwhelmed and didn't know what to do so I said a prayer at the altar and told my husband I wanted to leave. I have been back to the Holy Hill three times since then and have not experienced that same feeling again.

My next visit to Dr. Haik and Dr. Ainbinder was in November, 1992. At that time they told me the cancer was gone, this was less than four months after my treatment. Dr.

Haik said another doctor looking into my eye would not be able to tell I had every had a problem.

I believe that my eye was healed in October on the Holy Hill and I attribute my cure to the power of prayer and to my faith in God. My family and friends and I prayed very hard for this miracle and we are extremely grateful to Jesus and to His Holy Mother for their loving care of me.

I should add that the doctors said even though the cancer was gone, they could not guarantee I would not lose my sight in the left eye because of the radiation treatment. At this time, I have some trouble reading small print or reading for a long time as well as doing other close work, but I can drive my car and do almost anything else I want to do.

My husband and I returned to Conyers in December and I was privileged to be allowed in the Apparition Room on December 13. During the Apparition, I witnessed very bright flashing light over the statue of Our Loving Mother and over the Crucifix about the fireplace. My husband took some awesome pictures outside and we have shown them to family and friends. My granddaughter's Rosary, which was among many I had taken with me to be blessed by the Blessed Mother, turned golden.

This testimony would be incomplete without a statement concerning my spiritual life. By the grace of God I was granted a physical healing. Also by His grace my spiritual life has changed. My faith, which has been the strength that saw me through the many difficulties of life has grown even deeper. My prayer life has become richer and I have resumed the practice of monthly confession. My ability to reach out to other people has increased. As a teacher (retired), I feel a desire to teach about The Mass and my pastor has suggested a way to accomplish this. Again, by the grace of God, I will be able to reach that goal.

> Margaret D. Laurent
> Norco, Louisiana
> February 22, 1993

[In another correspondence, Mrs. Laurent commented, "I heard something. . .that I did not realize. St. Lucy's feast day is December 13, she is the patron saint for eye problems and she is also my Confirmation patron saint. That's exciting to me."]

Letter from Barrett G. Haik, M.D.

February 22, 1993

Ms. Margaret H. Laurent
301 Sixth Street
Norco, LA 70079

R e:Ms. Margaret H. Laurent
TMC #: 04230207

Dear Margaret:
It was such a pleasure to speak with you on February 22, 1993. I understand from our conversation that you are participating in an effort to compile a book of miraculous cures. We would certainly place your remarkable response to therapy in that category. We will continue to watch closely and pray with you that your cure from melanoma is long-standing.

In the meantime, may this find you well as always.

Warmest regards,
Barrett G. Haik, M.D.
Department of Ophthalmologic
Oncology and Orbital Disease

BGH/401
DD: 2/22/93
DT: 2/23/93
822.01

Testimony of Maria L. Iglesias:

In June of 1991, following a number of outpatient clinic visits and having undergone a series of diagnostic tests at the Metropolitan Hospital and Medical Center in New York City, a facility of the NYC Health and Hospitals Corporation, I was diagnosed as suffering from Third Stage Ovarian Cancer.

In August of 1991, I was admitted to Bellevue Hospital and Medical Center, another facility of the NYC/HHC, whose medical services are provided by the New York University School of Medicine—recognized as one of the leading oncological research and treatment centers of the United States. After further tests and reconfirmation of the original diagnosis, I undertook a treatment program consisting of the following: major surgery which took place in early September of 1991 followed by six months of chemotherapy beginning in the month of October of 1991 and concluding in March of 1992.

Following the conclusion of the chemotherapy program, I was scheduled for a Cat-Scan and blood work every three months to determine if there was a resurgence of my condition. The Cat-Scan and blood work for the month of June 1992 showed no change in my condition, that is to say, everything appeared calm.

At the urging of friends and family, I made plans to visit Conyers, Georgia, in September of 1992, the site of the monthly apparition of the Virgin Mary, to give thanks for the blessings I had received. I was scheduled to leave for Georgia the day following the Cat-Scan and blood work to be performed on me at Bellevue Hospital and Medical Center. Those tests were performed as scheduled, however, no results were available prior to me leaving for Conyers, Georgia.

Upon arriving at Conyers, those ministering at the site were advised of my condition and my fears and hopes with respect to full remission of the ovarian cancer. As a consequence, I was invited to remain in the Apparition Room, during the period when Our Blessed Virgin was expected to appear. Although I do not claim to have seen Our Holy Mother at that time, I did see what appeared to be some flashes of light and underwent a profound spiritual experience.

Upon my return to New York City I found a letter from the Bellevue Hospital and Medical Center urging me to come in for a medical consultation. When I did so, I was advised that the September Cat-Scan had indicated a recurrence of the cancerous condition. An additional and more intense program of chemotherapy was recommended and arrangements were made to admit me the following week to begin the treatment. Again at the urging of my family, to whom I had recounted my experience at Conyers, prior to undergoing this new treatment I insisted upon having another Cat-Scan done along with the accompanying blood work.

TO THE APPARENT CONSTERNATION OF THE MEDICAL AND ONCOLOGICAL STAFF OF THE HOSPITAL, THIS CAT-SCAN AND CORRESPONDING BLOOD WORK INDICATED ABSOLUTELY NO PRESENCE OF CANCER IN MY BODY. The Chief of Service, an internationally recognized oncologist, was called in to consult and he confirmed—after physical (hands-on) diagnosis—the results of the latest Cat-Scan. The new treatment program was thereupon cancelled, although reluctantly by some hospital staff. The normally scheduled Cat-Scan performed in December of 1992 AGAIN SHOWED ME TO BE FREE OF ANY CAN-

CEROUS PRESENCE.

In October of 1992 I returned to Conyers, Georgia, accompanied by my brother-in-law, Mr. Rudy Garcia, to give thanks to Our Blessed Virgin Mother, and he, too underwent a profound spiritual experience.

It is with an unwavering belief that at Conyers, Georgia, in September of 1992, I received the Blessing of Healing from Our Holy Mother of God, that I offer this testimony, giving thanks to Her for interceding with God the Father on my behalf.

Maria L. Iglesias
Palisades Park, NJ

Hospital Progress Report

Patient: Iglesias, Maria
1271881

TO WHOM IT MAY CONCERN:

Ms. Maria Iglesias was admitted to Bellevue Hospital on 9/30/92-10/2/92 due to a 3-4 cm. mass on the vaginal cuffs s/p TAW/B50, 6 cycles of chemo for ov CA stage IIIB. Patient had had CT's up until 9/92 when mass identified. Patient had CT _____ _____ on 10/1/92 which was non-diagnostic. No cancer cells seen.

Patient examined by Dr. Wallach, GYN oncologist on 10/2/92 and obvious mass noted. Decision made to D/C on 10/2/92 and have patient return on 10/26/92 for repeat abd/pelvic CT 10/27/92.

If canceled, please call Dr. Lowers, GYN.

Testimony of Rudy Garcia

I, Rudy Garcia, am an experienced journalist based in New York city, N.Y. I am by nature and profession skeptical and often downright cynical. On the other hand, my experience also has taught me there often occur unexplained and unexplainable phenomena which leave no alternative but to accept by faith. The following is my testimony as to what I, personally, experienced in Conyers, Georgia, in mid-October of 1992.

122

After more than a year of treatment and follow-up care for third stage ovarian cancer, my sister-in-law, Ms. Maria L. Iglesias, went to Conyers, Georgia, in mid-September of 1992, at the urging of friends and family. A devout Catholic, she had heard of the monthly apparition of the Virgin Mary at that location and intended to go to give thanks for the blessings already received and to pray for continued health. Unbeknownst to her, a Cat-Scan taken at Bellevue Hospital Medical Center in New York City the day before she left had indicated a return of her cancerous condition. When she returned to New York she recounted having undergone a profound spiritual experience in the Apparition Room while at Conyers.

As a result of the positive readings of the Cat-Scan, the medical staff at Bellevue ordered a new and more intense chemotherapy program for Maria. At the urgings of her family and friends, to whom she had related her experience at Conyers, she insisted on having another Cat-Scan done prior to commencing the new chemo program. The results of this second Cat-Scan showed her to be clear of any cancerous presence and chemotherapy was suspended. She immediately expressed an interest in returning to Conyers for the October apparition of the Virgin, to give thanks and to offer her testimony. She asked me to accompany her to help with the driving and expenses, which I did.

While at Conyers, having nothing else to do, I accompanied Maria to Mass on the morning of the scheduled apparition. I must note here that, although raised a Catholic, except for certain ceremonial occasions, funerals and the like, I had not attended Mass in more than 40 years and had not gone to Confession in nearly 45 years. During the Mass, while thinking and speculating on what had occurred with Maria and her health, I was overwhelmed by a profound sense of sadness along with great agitation. I could not explain what was happening until suddenly I knew with extraordinary certainty that I could not achieve peace unless I reconciled with Our Holy Mother and the Church. Immediately upon conclusion of the Mass I "waylaid" a priest assigned to that Conyers parish and expressed my absolute need that he hear my confession, the first I had made in 45 years.

I should note here that tears were streaming down my face during the latter portion of the Mass and, of course, during my confession. However, after confessing and performing my Penance, an extraordinary peace came over me. I accompanied Maria to the Apparition site in Conyers and prayed in thanks the rest of the day. At her urging I also gave my testimony to those present on that occasion. Since, I have maintained my reconciliation with the Church and adhered to its rites and tenets, secure in my faith. I have no doubt but that it was the hand of Our Blessed Virgin Mary which touched me and led to this reconciliation and do so attest and give thanks before God.

Rudy Garcia
New York, NY

Testimony of Sister Martha Rita Luckett:

An account of the healing of Sister Frances Patricia Clifford, age 86, who is retired at the Motherhouse of the Sisters of Charity of Nazareth, Kentucky as of September 1991.

Shortly after the return from my first visit to Conyers, Georgia (Nov. 12, 13, 14) I happened to come upon Sister Frances Patricia who was very nauseated and in need of help. After bathing her face, I proceeded to help her to her room. Leaving her, I immediately returned with some of the specially blessed water from Nancy's well. Instructing Sister to apply the water, recite seven Our Fathers, seven Hail Mary's, seven Glory Be's and the Apostles' Creed, I promised to join my prayers with hers. Thus began a very warm and confidential friendship. Sister was most diligent in following the given advice. In the days to follow, when questioned about her condition, she insisted that she was better day by day.

Previous to Sister's coming to live with me at our Motherhouse, her doctor in Columbus, Ohio had told her that a scan had revealed a tumor on her ovary and advised surgery but she refused consent. Being advised to come to the Motherhouse to live, Sister Mary Patricia, our registered nurse, insisted the Sister see Dr. Kemple in Louisville. He reported an abdominal mass but that surgery was not advised. Since nothing more could be done, Sister was dismissed. Our Sister nurse then sent her to Dr. Anderson at Flaget Hospital in Bardstown, Kentucky. He advised a scan which revealed the tumor and requested all records from Mt. Carmel Hospital in Columbus, Ohio. This last scan showed that the tumor had grown three inches or more. Surgery was advised and this time Sister consented. On January 27, 1992, the tumor was removed with no trace of cancer. She was back home in a day or so. The doctor was somewhat mystified.

Now, almost three months have passed and no negative signs have come to the fore. Sister continues to use the specially blessed water and to say the assigned prayers. She is thoroughly convinced her cure is due to prayer and strong faith. God be praised and thanked!

Since it was decided at Conyers that I write up this beautiful case, we have requested diagnostic reports from her doctor (please see enclosures).

Realizing her very special blessing, Sister Frances

Patricia spends much of her time sharing the beautiful and God-willed experience. For any sick Sisters whom she encounters, an immediate request is made for some specially blessed water to be given, along with the above suggested prayers. Surely Our Lady is very pleased with her quiet and constant promotion of so worthy a cause.

> Submitted by—
> Sister Martha Rita Luckett
> Nazareth Motherhouse
> Nazareth, Kentucky

Testimony of Mary Joan Freese:

January 30

Our Loving Mothers Children

You have my permission to put my letter from Dr. Zellner or whatever you want in the book, etc.

I thank you, God and Our Loving Mother for everything you have done for me.

I have also had a spiritual Healing.

Since I came down in June and July, my sister, niece, daughter and her three small children have gone back to church. Thank God.

> Your friend in Christ,
> Mary (Joan) Freese
> Lawrenceburg, Indiana

November 1, 1992

Mrs. Mary Joan Freese
19315 Parr Drive
Lawrenceburg, IN 47025

Dear Joan:

I recently received the reports of your chest x-ray and blood work and knew you would be interested in them.

The chest x-ray was compared with the one done in July. There has been no change. There is no evidence of active disease. There are post-surgical changes, but these remain stable.

A battery of liver function studies was obtained and all values are normal.

The complete blood counts were obtained and all values are within normal limits.

I think you were interested in a summary of your experience with the lung cancer, so I will try to give you that in the next few paragraphs.

We first saw you at the Barrett Center on September 10, 1990. You had no symptoms of lung cancer at that time. Your history indicated a scar in the right lung of at least three years duration. Dr. Beverly Carpenter, who was managing your arthritis, had gotten routine chest x-ray and CTs of the chest over the previous three years. The lung cancer was discovered on the CT of the chest which was done routinely in August, 1991. You were referred to Dr. David Wiltse who performed bronchoscopy and biopsied the mass in your lung. This biopsy revealed the presence of cancer.

A report CT scan of your chest revealed the presence of a 4 x 4 cm mass in the right upper lobe, two mediastinal lymph nodes appeared to be involved, one in the right peritracheal area and one in the left prevascular area.

A bone scan revealed abnormal uptake in the right fourth and sixth ribs. The appearance of this uptake and your history suggested this was due to recent traumatic fracture. A CT scan of your head showed no evidence of metastatic disease to the brain. At this point, your lung cancer stage was III-B.

Several options for management were discussed, among which was the possibility of entering a study protocol through which you would receive concomitant radiation and chemotherapy over a five-week period. At the end of that time you would be re-evaluated for surgery. You elected to enter the study program.

On September 23, 1991, your chemotherapy and radiation therapy treatments were initiated. Over the next five weeks you received daily radiation treatments, except for Saturday and Sunday, to the right upper chest and mediastinum. You received one week of chemotherapy at the beginning of your radiation treatment and at the end of your radiation treatment. Each week this consisted of two doses of Cisplatin, a week apart, and five consecutive days of VP-16.

You experienced a lot of difficulty during this five-week period of treatment. There was a lot of nausea and vomiting and periods of dehydration and postural hypotension. You did make it through and your final treatment was on October 5, 1991. After a period of weeks for you to get back on your feet, you were re-evaluated with scans and x-rays. The repeat CT scan of your chest showed a marked reduction in the size of the right lung cancer and complete disappearance of the nodes in the mediastinum. Your repeat bone scan showed no change from the previous one. Your repeat CT scan of the head showed no change.

You elected to proceed with surgical removal of the residual cancer in your right lung. This was accomplished on December 3, 1991. Dr. Reising removed the right upper lobe of your lung, and with it the residual cancer. He also removed all the nodes he could find in the mediastinum. Pathology reported residual, moderate to poorly differentiated adenocarcinoma of 1.5 cms in diameter. There were two nodes positive for metastatic adenocarcinoma in the lobar chain and one in the right peritracheal chain.

During the recovery period from your surgery, you were admitted to the hospital with a severe urinary tract infection. You responded nicely to antibiotics and were discharged on the 28th of December, 1991.

According to the study protocol, since there was residual tumor, you were supposed to undergo an additional eight days of radiation therapy and two courses of chemotherapy. Since you were having so much difficulty recuperating from the treatment already received, you elected on the sixth of January, 1992 to forego any further treatment.

Over the past ten months, you have slowly improved. You have regained about 20 of the 30 pounds that you lost with treatment. Your mental outlook has improved markedly. Your stamina and respiratory reserve continue to improve. Your most recent blood and x-ray studies reveal no evidence of recurrence of your cancer at this time. We need, however, to keep a close eye on things, so that should there be a recurrence, we have the option of doing something about it as soon as possible.

I hope the above information is useful to you.

Sincerely,
David C. Zellner, M.D.

DCZ/car

D:11/02/92
T:11/04/92

Reflections: Diary of a Pilgrim

February 15, 1993

I returned to Conyers, Georgia, on February 10, 1993, to review medical testimonies of healed pilgrims. I was privileged to be present for the February 13th apparition and I felt especially blessed to stay at the home of Janie and Collin McIsaac in Conyers. I had just met Janie and her lovely family in November.

Janie is a living example of unconditional love. She is an inspiration to all who know her and there are many. She has four children of her own who have a special love for Mary and her precious Son. These children proudly wear the cross of St. Benedict over their school clothes even though they have been pressured to do otherwise by school educators. What courage!

Janie's home is always full of children. Anyone who asks her assistance receives it. There are rarely less than thirteen for dinner. The door is always open and each is welcome. Each is treated as family. Janie works daily to accommodate the thousands of pilgrims who came to Conyers. I have watched her wash Nancy's floors, answer phones, do laundry and even give Nancy Fowler's dog "Happy Girl" a bath. She looks for opportunities to serve, and has even shared with me that her greatest pain is when Nancy insists she rest and take time away from Our Loving Mother's ministry. Janie never complains. She smiles constantly and I've been with her at 3:00 a.m. in her home when she was joyfully sharing and rinsing a few more dishes that constantly fill her sink.

Janie's husband, Collin, seems to understand the magnitude of his wife's work for and devotion to Christ. He never complains about the multitude of people who come and go and dine at his home. You never hear him mention or complain of having no privacy.

The McIsaacs live the messages being delivered at Conyers. They live them with love and joy and acceptance. This family is a lamp in today's darkness.

Janie had helped in the effort to arrange for my presence in the Apparition Room on February 13, 1993. The purpose for this, of course, was to enhance credibility for this modest literary effort. Janie dropped me off that Saturday morning and I was to participate in the preparation for the pilgrims for the noon apparition.

Close to noon, the Apparition Room was packed with terminally ill pilgrims from all over America. A woman from New York named Joan Cashon came from the outside into the room of apparitions to share her blessings from Christ and His Mother. Joan has suffered immeasurably from her long battle with cancer. As I listened, my eyes filled, then overflowed. My heart was so touched. I stood up and offered her my seat, which she insisted she could not accept. I did not take no for an answer. As I started to leave, another woman said "Please, you are supposed to be here; take my seat."

I asked, "Are you ill?" The woman commented that she has liver cancer, but she was going to kneel and praise God. I knew I could not stay in this room any longer. I did not belong there. I felt humbled, grateful, full of pain and full of love. . .all at one time. The tears poured down my face. The Lord had blessed me and reminded me of my good health. I was reminded that Jesus is everywhere and that there are no walls. I went out to the porch and James Tsakanikas from Clifton, Va., placed me in a chair right next to the open window on the front of the farmhouse. . .opposite Nancy Fowler. . .right next to a small boy praying the rosary. What was to happen next has become a permanent part of my heart and faith.

As the visionary began to pray, I looked up. Through the open window, I saw a great light over the crucifix at the front of the room. I was totally captured and so filled with love that I haven't words to express it. I felt a tugging on my jacket and I looked down. The little boy seated next to me was so excited. He had lights—bright lights in every bead of his white plastic rosary beads. The lights seemed to momentarily distract people's attention within the Apparition Room.

When Nancy said, "The Blessed Mother is departing," the crowds gasped, raised their arms and some knelt. Lights were flashing on and off inside and outside the farmhouse. Our Blessed Lady was calling us all to attention with this magnificent light show. Thousands were witness to this. The Lord was reminding us of our journey back to Him. What a grace!

February 25, 1993

It is amazing how the Lord turns an ordinary day into a spectacular event for Him. I've learned that there are no ordinary days when we choose Him. Each day becomes a joy.

I have experienced a little difficulty with mobility in my right arm and shoulder for some time. February 25th, I decided to so something about it, since I had been asked by Dr. Miranda Shaw to speak at The University of Richmond on the topic of apparitions that evening.

I drove across town, reached a familiar stop light where I was to turn right. I turned left, and felt some annoyance with myself. I thought, as I pulled into The Picket Fence Boutique. . ."OK, I'll turn a negative into a positive. I do need a birthday gift for a friend." The usually perky blonde, Sue, greeted me inside the boutique. She seemed, however, preoccupied, and I felt a sadness for her. I thought, "What can I do to make her day a little better?" I went back to my car and pulled some of the pictures taken in Conyers and I showed her the medical testimonies of people healed of cancer. She proceeded to tell me that a family member had cancer and had just yesterday taken a turn for the worse. She commented on how upset she was. I reached in my purse and found a picture of Our Loving Mother and a miraculous medal blessed at Conyers. I gave these to her and noticed that something fell out of my bag. It was a prayer to St. Peregrine, Patron Saint of malignant tumors. I gave this to her as well. She then said, "I know She sent you here today."

Two days later I was to see a neighbor who lives a few miles down the road. I have not seen her in years and passed her in the grocery store the evening before Richmond's predicted four inches of snow. She volunteers at St. Mary's Hospital, where my husband has served on the board. I felt compelled to say hi and reached in my pocket to find one blessed miraculous medal. I gave it to her and wished her well. She commented that I would never know what it meant to her and that she could not speak of it, but would tell me someday.

I picked up my groceries somewhat puzzled and left happy. A friend of mine, Peggy Harris, called me at home and asked for prayers for the woman I had seen in the grocery store. Peggy commented that the distant neighbor was going into the hospital early the next morning for a radical mastectomy. Peggy asked me to pray for a safe trip (because of the predicted snow) and for a successful operation. I found myself saying a quiet "Thank you, Jesus." I am convinced that miracles are only miracles because we don't believe they can happen. They should be part of the normal course of events and they are!

March 3, 1993

I woke up this morning to a grey sky and a gentle rain. Rainy days are usually blamed for my getting a slow start and engaging in a little procrastination, but today my heart is so full, and I feel so humble and grateful. I know how blessed I am to be here. I know what a gift life is and can be for all of us, and one woman has served to teach me more in a moment than a host of university professors.

I met Joan Cashon and her husband Lou on the afternoon of February 12th on the back porch of the farmhouse in Conyers, Georgia. I do not believe in accidental meetings. I do believe that everything is in Divine Order, and that Joan was sent to me by God to increase my capacity for love. How great He is.

Last night I opened the mail late and found a letter from Joan. I have chosen to include this for reasons which will be obvious to us all. I was privileged to be able to give up my seat in the Apparition Room to Joan. I was moved to do so by The Holy Spirit. While Joan had driven all the way from New York, she never asked to be in that room on February 13th. As I looked around and saw all the sick and severely handicapped people, my eyes overflowed with tears. I was suddenly conscious as never before of all the gifts the good Lord has given me. My eyes and vision are perfect. My arms and legs take me everywhere I choose to go. Other than four Caesarian sections, I have never had any operations. How many times had I thanked the Lord for what I took for granted?

My dear Joan, I could never give back to you what you have given to me. Your strength makes me stronger. Your love warms my heart. Your faith is deeply etched in my memory. How very much you are loved and appreciated. You are a finely tuned instrument being used by Him, and I am grateful for your letter. You inspire me to work harder.

February 25, 1993
Blooming Grove, New York

Dear Ann Marie,
I must thank you again for the beautiful grace of being in the Apparition Room in Conyers. I am asking God to bless you for your generosity of spirit. *Meeting you* was a special blessing for Lou and me. I've enclosed a picture of us together, but I don't need that to remember your beautiful green eyes and lovely smile.

We have been very busy since we saw you. A dear friend in Florida died and we were able to spend the last two days of her life together. She was a gallant lady and her funeral mass was truly a testament to the Living Christ.

You asked that I share my story with you and I will attempt to do so. In the Fall of 1990 I was diagnosed as having ovarian cancer. I was operated on at New York Hospital, Cornell Medical Center, on October 16, 1990. Dr. Caputo, head of gynecological oncology, was my surgeon. He felt I had a good chance of recovery and I was sent home to receive an eight month dose of a moderate chemotherapy treatment as "insurance." I took the treatments under the care of Dr. Hal Teitelbaum in Horton Hospital in Middletown, New York. By June of 1991, we thought it was behind us.

In the summer and early Fall of 1991, began experiencing aches in my back and shoulders which I attributed to the radical hysterectomy I had undergone. In September, the discomfort escalated and Dr. Teitelbaum began tests for osteoarthritis. When all the results came back negative, he scheduled me for CAT Scans of my pelvis, abdomen and chest. Those tests revealed a liver tumor and multiple tumors in the median area of my chest. Before they can treat a cancer, they have to know the primary source, and so I began a series of procedures to pinpoint the primary. (Those procedures included three needle biopsies of my liver, a mediastinoscopy on my chest and finally liver surgery.) While waiting for results I had a metaport implanted in my chest to facilitate whatever chemotherapy lay in store.

On December 3, 1991, I went to have the stitches removed from the metaport implant and while in the doctor's office I began to go numb, beginning with my feet and working up toward my diaphragm. Leaving his office, I went directly to Dr. Teitelbaum. He examined me and told me the following: (1) I might be dying; (2) I would probably never move again; (3) I almost certainly would never walk; and (4) the only way to save my life was to begin massive doses of steroids immediately and to send me by ambulance to Memorial Hospital—Sloan Kettering.

I remained in Sloan Kettering through Christmas, receiving steroid treatments and radiation for the spinal tumor they discovered with an M.R.I. I went home just before New Years Day 1992 and by mid-January, I received my answer to all the tests done to try to find out what kind of cancer I was battling. Approximately ten percent of all cancer patients have an undiagnosed primary. As I understand it, those undiagnosed cases fall into two larger and one very small category. I fell into the smallest area (.8 percent)—a category with a very anaplastic, virulent description. Dr. Teitelbaum told me that Sloan had a treatment for undiagnosed cancers, but that he could only hold out to me a fifty-percent chance that I would have any response to it. He originally planned six treatments (although we stopped at four), but after two treatments he would scan me again. If the results were not promising, he would stop treatments because at that point the quality of my life had to be considered. I received six hours of chemotherapy a day for five days. After two treatments, the scans showed a dramatic improvement. I started my final treatment on April 28, 1992. Those four stays in the hospital took longer than the five days of actual treatment. I was quite ill and the stays ranged from eight to nineteen days a piece.

[In addition to my illness, Lou and I have had other

difficulties. While I was hospitalized for my last treatment, my mother died (May 11th) and I was not permitted out to attend a funeral. I was released a week later and Lou's sister Queenie lost her battle with cancer on May 27th, 1992. Lou's only other sister also has cancer and we had to put Lou's mom in a nursing home in September of '92. She died in February of '93.]

My scans in May showed my chest to be totally free of tumors, the spinal tumor had disappeared (spinal cord and bond damage still were evident on the M.R.I.) and there remained only a small spot on my liver. The doctor feels that if the "spot" were active disease, it should have begun to grow by now.

I started walking in December of '91 with a rolling walker and a nurse holding a sheet around me to keep me upright. I then graduated to a regular walker and then to a four-pronged cane. My balance and spinal strength have so improved that I no longer use even the cane. My doctor told me that anyone who has experienced the kind of paralysis I did, is usually dead within a month. No one expected the kind of spinal regeneration I have experienced. The doctor also says that he cannot tell me I am in remission. I have a rare and malignant cancer and he cannot predict whether this will last a day, a month or a year.

That is my medical history. My spiritual journey bears recounting. Only with the Grace of God and the help of Our Loving Mother have Lou and I been able to walk the path on which we found ourselves. (After nine childless years of marriage, my mother promised Our Lady that if she had a little girl, she would give her back to her. Never knowing that until the last few years, I consecrated myself to Jesus through Mary using the Demontfort consecration when I was fourteen years old. So you can see, she has always been my Loving Mother!) We have been strengthened and blessed through the prayers of friends and strangers alike.

When in the hospital for my first of the four chemo treatments in 1992, Lou made a phone contact with Sister Breige McKenna in Florida. She prayed with me, reminding me that nothing was impossible with God. She also suggested that I pray to Padre Pio and ask his intercession for my healing. Through the Upper Room Prayer group to which we belong, I met Barbara O'Malley, which has a healing ministry based in Illinois. In September of '92, I was strong enough to make a pilgrimage to Scottsdale, Arizona. At Maria Goretti parish, Father Jack Spaulding and a group of young people are receiving messages from Jesus and His Mother. Several of them prayed with us and then we were privileged to be in the home of Reyes and Estella Ruez while Estella received an apparition of Our Lady. A rosary that had been placed in Padre Pio's mitten was given to me to hold during a mass we attended in Phoenix at a Marian Conference. We returned home from a grace-filled week in the latter part of September. I began reading the books from Conyers, given to me months earlier by a friend. I was very interested and asked Our Lady to bring us there if it would please Her Son. I thought a pilgrimage of thanksgiving would be appropriate in the light of all the graces we were receiving. I didn't mention my desire to Lou, but I hoped to be in Conyers on the thirteenth of October. I put it all in God's hands and without planning or preparation we found ourselves en route to Georgia.

It came to me that it would be the seventy-fifth anniversary of the last Fatima Apparition and I was elated. Lou and I both saw the sun "spinning" and we knew this was a special place. Our Lady brought me into the Apparition Room and Lou was allowed to stay with me. It was a day filled with graces for the two of us. I bless myself daily with the water from Nancy's well and wear a miraculous medal put "in faith" on the altar in her yard. The day after the public apparition I was privileged to have Nancy pray with me. She said that she "felt strongly" that I should ask Padre Pio to intercede for my healing. (I have asked the good Padre in prayer to be my spiritual father and I continue to ask his prayers.)

I have since given up my cane and my back seems to grow in strength each week. I have minor discomforts due to nerve damage, but my balance is almost back to normal. The length of time for which I can stand or walk continues to increase.

With permission from my doctor (because visits to him haven't been more than three weeks apart) we embarked on a five week vacation. We stopped in Conyers for the February apparition and, through your generosity, I was again permitted in the Apparition Room. We're hoping to be in Conyers on March 13, on the last leg of our trip back to New York State.

We are on a journey of faith. The holiness is the center of my life. It is there that I believe, Jesus, the Healer, touches us. He has also chosen to gift me with what I believe is the presence of His Mother in Conyers. Saint Joseph, Saint Michael and Padre Pio are among the many friends who have strengthened and prayed for us on this walk. I nourish myself at the Lord's table and through His Holy Word in scripture. I have prayed for and received excellent medical care.

When I first heard the word "cancer," I thought of the story of the man born blind in John, Chapter Nine. His disciples asked Jesus, "Rabbi, who sinned, this man or his parents, that he was born blind?" Jesus answered, *"Neither he nor his parents sinned; it is so that the works of God might be made visible through him. "* I asked that this might be true of my illness. I do not know God's plan for my life—but, I do know that He is a God of Love and Mercy. He is teaching

Lou and me to live in the present moment, trusting in His infinite love.

Please pray for us, as we do for you. We'll be back in Blooming Grove on March fifteenth. On the sixteenth, I will have pelvic, abdominal and thoracic CAT scans taken. On the seventeenth an M.R.I. on my spine will be done. On the nineteenth, I will visit the doctor and we will evaluate the test results. I'll drop you a line to "update" my status. Lou and I wish you all of God's blessings on your book and Our Loving Mother's protection over your whole life.

Love and Prayers,
Joan

March 6, 1993

I thought this book would be finished long ago, but Our Loving Mother guides my heart and my hand and she is not finished. Each day is a powerful testimony to His Love. One such witness is the man James Tsakanikas from Clifton, Virginia. I met him in Conyers, Georgia, when a group of people devoted to Christ prayed together. I was seated next to James and was overwhelmed by all the beautiful signs Our Loving Father had given me through His Holy Mother. I didn't want anyone to know how emotional I felt when James lovingly invoked the Holy Spirit. "One of our sisters is overwhelmed. . .send her Your Peace." My body was on fire and the tears fell uncontrollably from my eyes. I don't think I will ever forget that moment.

James' knowledge of his faith is overwhelming. The courage of his convictions is unfailing. James made me aware that there were pieces missing in my faith. As a Catholic, I assumed that I was always given what I needed. It never occurred to me to seek or that sometimes we are given incorrect information. I've learned when some things don't feel right or don't resonate within. . .there is usually a good reason. James was quick to point out that those who profess the Catholic faith are involved in a Theocracy *not* a democracy. Catholics answer to Rome and are not entitled to adopt their own agendas unless they make another faith choice. I've learned we need to ask and seek and we shall find. This sounds familiar, doesn't it? We need to accept some responsibility for our faith regardless of what faith we profess. We need to be informed and informed correctly.

James gave me his precious Mother Seton relic. I was very moved and emotional. The Blessed Mother was present for this. My entire home. . . up and down was filled with the strong scent of bouquets of roses. What a beautiful gift! What a beautiful moment.

I must also add—it takes courage to speak out when you are only one, but the feeling of freedom that comes from the knowledge of truth is more than worth it. I thank James Tsankanikas for his support and friendship, also for his courage.

April 3, 1993

There are two people who must be remembered, not because they desire it, but rather it is the wish of all who know Bernie and Bob Hughes. I personally feel a closeness to them because their names come up repeatedly in the same breath as the word Conyers. It is hard, if not impossible, to speak of the apparitions in Georgia without referencing this dynamic twosome.

I have asked two appropriate people to discuss their contributions. The first is known to you, as is the second. . .Nancy Fowler and George Collins.

When I asked Nancy to help share the love of Bob and Bernie Hughes, she didn't know where to begin, and so she left the task to the Holy Spirit who shared this and guided Nancy's pen:

> There are no words to express the thank you that's in my heart for your total dedication to God. When I think of your generous hearts, it brings tears to my eyes. You have set no limits to God and you have allowed God to work completely in your lives. Everyone you have encountered you have left the imprint of Christ within their hearts and we all have felt the warm embrace of Our Mother's arms through both of you. Our Mother says, *"I love you dearly."* Thank you. God bless you always.

> — Nancy Fowler

I mentioned that George Collins seemed to be the appropriate one to share the Hughes' contributions to Conyers. George records the messages of Our Lord and Our Loving Mother for Nancy. George is untiring in his devotion to God and His commitment to help Nancy. He has also been untiring in helping me with this literary effort.

Here in George Collins' words is a Conyers tribute to Bob and Bernie Hughes:

> Bob and Bernie Hughes are special people. Jesus had told Nancy before they came to Conyers. Jesus asked Nancy to have several people talk to them and help them. He did not

say why. Bob and Bernie had been to Medjugorje several times. Bob said before this he would go to church just in case there was a God.

They came down and began helping. Their warm, gentle hearts helped provide a source of gentleness and strength. Bob's calm sense of getting things done in business was needed. He began helping by putting his experience in getting things accomplished to work. When Bob and Bernie could see that the visions were authentic they began making plans to turn their successful business over to their sons. They began working full time for Jesus and His Mother in Conyers.

They gave up the security of running a successful business. Jesus said, *"Time is a gift."* They began giving their time to God, spreading the Conyers' messages from Jesus and Mary.

Immediately, Bob and Bernie were used by Jesus. Later, Bob and Bernie gave up running their business. Jesus began blessing them with more and more work. Their faith and sacrifices were being rewarded. Bob and Bernie bought the "farm," the thirty-acre site of the present apparitions of Our Loving Mother.

Bob and Bernie began committing more and more of their resources. They bought miraculous medals to give away and books to make available to pilgrims. They made rosaries freely available to the pilgrims.

The farm proved not to be big enough to handle the crowds. Property had to be rented for parking. Bob tried to use more and more of his resources to provide needed property.

Bob and Bernie have been blessed with some spiritual gifts from God. They can see the light around the crucifix during apparitions, also around those who are letting Jesus use them.

Their unselfishness and sacrifices are inspiring to others in the ministry because they give all that they have. They give their time and their money, but most of all their hearts. They have given up running their business to work for Jesus and Mary. They have given up the money that was their retirement fund and security. They have maintained their peace and gentleness and are humble. You can see they give for the sake of Jesus and are looking only to serve His Will. Once they discern what His Will is they do not withhold their time or resources.

It is because they maintain their littleness in the background that Jesus has given them more and more to do for Him. Their spiritual gifts have grown.

Bob and Bernie are examples of how humility and selflessness are rewarded by God. The giving natures of Bob and Bernie are an example for all to follow.

May 15, 1993

Bishop Tony Nepomuceno of the Phillipines addressed the 1992 Marian Conference in Chicago. He made at least two references to Nancy Fowler and Conyers, Georgia. The Bishop pointed out that he visited Conyers in September 1992 while traveling to Florida. He said, "I was amazed by the huge multitudes of people coming from all over the United States making a pilgrimage there." He referred to the messages received by Nancy on November 13, 1991, when Our Blessed Mother asked, *"Are you listening?. . .Think about the goodness of God. Be thankful. "* Bishop Nepomuceno also referred to the Conyers message of January 13, 1991: *"Sorrow reigns in Heaven over the many lost souls in the country. "*

It is of particular interest that the Bishop referred to Giana Talone, who experienced simultaneous visions with Nancy. (See testimony of Carol Ameché.)

[Bishop Nepomuceno's remarks were obtained from the tape of his Saturday and Sunday homilies at the 1992 Marian Conference, "My Soul Proclaims the Greatness of the Lord," Chicago Marian Center, 1847 W. Estes, Chicago, IL 60626.]

May 16, 1993

I woke up this morning contemplating the events at Conyers that took place during May. I was once again reminded that miracles are only miracles because we don't believe they can happen. They happen every day! I am so grateful and so humbled by the graces Jesus is pouring out at Conyers. I am evermore aware of His all-consuming love.

On May 15, I spent the day with Nancy going over this modest effort. Jesus confirmed to Nancy that He was asking me to be an instrument for Him—something I have felt in my heart for a long time and denied. It is still overwhelming for me to speak of. . .I know, however that *all* graces come from Him and without Him we are nothing. Nancy Fowler is the first to say that we are like brooms, and when Jesus is finished with us He will lovingly place us back in the closet.

I returned home and on June 15, Tuesday, hosted a rosary in my home for Our Loving Mother. I was asked by Robin Hickey to pray with her. I felt an instant overwhelming love for her as a child of God. The following is her testimony of what took place. Thank you, Jesus. Thank you, Mary. Please Jesus always keep me little for You. Thy will. . .not mine!

* * * *

My name is Robin Hickey. I was born with Cerebral Palsy (CP) affecting my right side (right-hand leg and foot smaller) and both eyes (right eye half-blind). In August 1992 I was diagnosed with Multiple Sclerosis (MS) causing fatigue, eye problems such as erratic movements and seeing a "blue dot" around most of the vision field of right eye.

On June 15, 1993, Ann Marie first prayed with me. I was crying, and I could feel the spirit descend into my body giving me a feeling of peace I hadn't had before. The next day my right hand was the same size as my left. The tiredness/fatigue that I had felt was gone. I also noticed that the stiffness I had awakened with each morning for about the past 2½ years and for which I had to exercise in order to relieve, was gone. The most drastic change was a change in behavior. For longer than I can recall I had been sad and angry and it showed in my treatment of others. The sadness and anger have gone and have been replaced by happiness and peace.

On July 5, 1993, I was examined by Dr. Bush, the neurologist I had seen for about seven years, first for the CP, then for the MS. When I showed him my hands, he looked surprised and said, "How did that happen?" I told him what was happening to me. Upon examination, he noted that I had improved dexterity in my right hand, my eyes seemed to be working better together, and that I appeared to be walking better.

On the 5th also I was prayed over again by Ann Marie. After this session I could feel something lengthening my leg. The spasticity that sometimes would cause my leg and arm to jump involuntarily is gone. . .

Driving home from work on June 15, 1993, I smelled the beautiful scent of roses. I continue to smell them daily. I thank the Blessed Mother and Jesus each day for the internal as well as the external miracle that I'm experiencing.

Wake Up America has taken eight months to deliver. It has been most difficult to write because of all the information that the author felt was necessary for completion. The book was not designed to embellish a series of extraordinary events.

I am a television interviewer and have spent several years in hard-nosed reporting. I am a debater and have even taught debate. This skill has served me well. I have. . .many times. . .played the Devil's Advocate with myself. I have made hundreds of phone calls and conducted as many interviews.

No one will deny something extraordinary is happening in Conyers, Georgia! People are returning their lives to God. The medical documentation bears witness to physical healings, referred to by doctors themselves as "miraculous." So you have seen.

The number of visitors has gone from five thousand pilgrims on the 13th of the month to an estimate of 80,000. One must ask why would eighty thousand people travel to a rural farm area forty miles west of Atlanta? Why do many return? Again and again? How does one explain the hundreds of unusual photographs taken at a simple farmhouse? Multitudes have smelled the roses. . .some have even taken this gift home with them. Why are statues bleeding and crying all over the world, but also at Conyers? Why would large numbers come to Conyers and stay outside in a freezing snowy blizzard? Why are people who have been to Conyers starting to pray? Why are some finding God for the first time? Why have hardened hearts softened? Why is bitterness replaced with love and forgiveness? Why is disbelief and skepticism rewarded with faith? Why are whole families returning to church after a weekend visit to the small place called Conyers? Why hasn't the lack of support from Rockdale officials hurt it or stopped it? Why hasn't an Archbishop's letter of disapproval brought it to an end? Why do world renowned-scientists affirm Conyers?

Wake Up America! Take Her Heart; Take Her Hand!

Ann Marie Hancock

More Urgent Messages From Around the World

The author humbly thanks Brother DePorres Stilp, MM, of Wilkes Barre, Pennsylvania, for the following compilation. Brother De-Porres works for Evangelization and funds are needed and donations are appreciated. He can be contacted at (717) 822-9925.

Mary: *". . .My children, you have not much time until My Son's Hand will come over the earth in justice. Convert. I beg you, while you still have time . . . "*

> February 28, 1988
> to Christina Gallagher from
> County Mayo, Ireland

MORE MESSAGES TO NANCY FOWLER OF CONYERS, GEORGIA

Jesus: *"Come into the palm of My hand. Think of the embryo. The embryo is completely dependent on its mother. Be completely dependent on me. Do not be independent but dependent. Dependence is greater freedom. With God, dependence is freedom. Freedom is to be free from the Evil One. The Evil One stirs up independence. 'Be liberated, be independent,' he says. 'Be a new man, a new woman.' Nothing is new in Satan. Everything is old and dark in Satan. You do not find freedom in Satan; rather you have bondage. Satan is master of one thing only—deception. In My second coming, there will be a new Heaven and a new earth. Everything will be made new. The old will be gone. Mankind is missing the signs of the times. When they miss the signs, they will wander and become lost; they will not find* *me. You have no time to yourself, for you are called to live for others. This calling comes from My God. There is a great deception occurring all over the world. My priests, My chosen elect will plunge into darkness, for very few are seeing the signs. "* [Nancy then had two visions. The first was of people walking into the light, a white light, whiter than any light on earth and they were at peace.]

Jesus: *"You have remained here physically; however, I brought your soul to first see the darkness, and then to see light. Tell others what I have shown you. "*

September 9, 1990

Jesus: *"The sins of mankind are offending the Holy Trinity of God. They are numerous and great and ever increasing. My Mother is growing weak from holding My hand back from striking. It pleases Me greatly when little souls come to console me, but they are too few. "*

September 10, 1990

Jesus: *"My children, My children have forced Me to bring a great punishment upon the earth. My Mother is mourning because many souls will be lost to me. Where are My Masses for Peace? The world does not want My mercy; well then, they shall not have My mercy. My people have ignored Me long enough. Understand now that My people will see the justice of God. A sign will be given in the heavens and My children will see this sign. When this sign is given, it will be too late to convert. Let those who are open hear Me. I am Jesus! I am the Son of God! I will not force man to love Me. I will not force My mercy upon man. "*

November 13, 1990

Jesus: *"Oh My foolish children, you do not know that I am God. Oh, if only My children would be children. If you block My graces here, then you will receive My punishment sooner. Woe be to the parishes that dishonor My Mother. If they dishonor My Mother, then they dishonor Me. I came through My Mother the first time, and so shall I come the second time. Let those who ignore My Mother know this: they are ignoring God. If you want to delay My punishment on* *this country, then come in numbers here and show Me your faith. "*

November 15, 1990

Jesus: *"Greater suffering will befall mankind. The Holy Trinity of God is deeply offended by the sins of mankind and the universal rejection of God. I am Jesus! I am one with the Father! I am the Second Person of the Blessed Trinity who speaks to you! The time is near. "*

December 29, 1990

Jesus: *"You are correct in saying My anger is mounting. My lost foolish children have ignored My Mother and Me enough. Everyone I have sent have My children ignored as well. Block My graces here and receive My punishment sooner. My children have failed to demonstrate any faith, any trust; they do not believe in our visits here. The time has come for My justice. My children do not believe in My justice, but they shall see My justice. I am giving the greatest graces here outside of My Mass. Nowhere are My graces being poured forth like they are here. Every one of My commandments are violated and abandoned. Murder! Murder! Murder is in their hearts! They murder the unborn! They murder the old! They murder the young! They murder the well! They murder the disabled! They slander My Name! They mock Me! I have given great signs from Heaven. Know they are grave signs. "*

December 30, 1990

Jesus: *"The Holy Spirit is a real Person just as I am. Trust the Holy Spirit as you trust your Jesus. I am imparting My wisdom of the Holy Trinity of God. To think less of the Holy Spirit is to think less of Me. Children, if you do not believe this, then you stand accused before Me. Then I say to you, you do not believe in the Holy Trinity of God. The entire world is in great darkness about this. Inspirations that come from the Holy Spirit of God are thrown away, discarded as so much trash in the gutter. Do not deny the Holy Spirit of God. If you do, I will deny you! Not to believe this is not to believe in Me, in God!"*

January 15, 1991

Mary: *"People of America, you will increase God's anger if you continue to ignore Jesus and Myself. I ask you from My sorrowful and mourning Heart to pray more for the salvation of souls. Your country is in the greatest danger, and you will not survive as a great nation any longer unless you are truly one nation under God. "*

January 16, 1991

Jesus: *"I have a message for all mankind. Stop trying to be greater than Me. Stop worshipping false gods! Stop murdering! Stop lying! Stop striking Me! Stop ignoring Me! Stop your selfish, egotistical ways! Begin anew—with sincere repentant hearts turn back to Me. Give Me your hearts of love. I am Jesus, Son of the Living God! My commandments of love are ways to help My children to grow in love with Me, in Me and through me. In America there are too many gods before Me!"*

January 17-19, 1991

Jesus: *"All of My children should rest on the Lord's Day. I want them to rest from all their worldly affairs and to take time to reflect upon My goodness and love. If they will do this, then they will appreciate My gifts more, for everything is a gift from Me. Then everything in their lives will be richer because they will see it from eyes of love. You will have time for your family, time for physical rest, time set aside for spiritual growth. Everything needs balance to work properly. Every human being is given a tiny seed of My perfect love. This seed is destined to grow in the fullness of My love. You cannot keep the Lord's Day holy unless you examine and improve yourselves and make amends for the sins committed during the previous six days. "*

February 9, 1991

Jesus: *"Many souls are freely choosing to live in darkness. They think their decision is just for a few years on this earth, but in actuality, it is for all eternity. Many souls are plunging into eternal fires and are damned for all times. Most are because of sins of the flesh. Those who willfully choose to murder are there with them. Repeated willful impure thoughts, words, and deeds are sending people to the eternal fires of darkness. Woe be this wicked generation!*

144

How quick you are to rationalize your sins and to no longer recognize them as sin. Violation of My Commandments kills the life of the soul. Woe to this wicked sinful generation! The anger of God the Father is mounting. Woe to My people who march with the murderers: the abortionists! Woe be My priests who engage in impure acts. "

March 22, 1991

Mary: *"Parents, please encourage your children to pray. Parents today are more concerned about their children excelling in worldly matters. If you are worldly parents, then your children will be worldly as well. If you love your children, then your children will love in return. Parents of the world, you are taking your responsibilities too lightly. My Son will hold you accountable. Be responsible about their spiritual, physical and emotional growth. But the greatest and most important of these three is spiritual growth because it is forever. American children are the most difficult of all. Many families put themselves above God. They exclude God in their lives. "*

March 30, 1991

Jesus: *"The Evil One counterfeits everything. He fishes and entraps men with juicy bait, and then they are hooked. Satan is the master of deception. He excels in pride and hatred. He glorifies only himself. Like a loving Father, I want to love and protect you all. Be on guard against those who come in sheep's clothing but inside are vicious wolves. They seek to destroy you. They masquerade as My servants. Do not be deceived by their fancy titles and worldly fame. I will help you if you will come to Me and ask for My help. In the days ahead, many will fall in My Church, and they will remain down because they will not come to Me for help. Many of My elect children are being deceived. Satan and evil spirits work extremely hard to destroy consecrated souls. No one, no one will succeed in battling Satan without My help! I say no one! The angels of Heaven would be helpless without My help. So also the saints would be so as well; yes, even the Mother of God herself, but she would never separate herself from God, for She is perfectly one with Him.*

December 10, 1990 and
March 26, 1991

Mary: *"My dear children of America and the world, you must stop offending God. Your souls are at stake, the very life of your souls. My children commit more sins now than at the time of Noah. I am crying for all the lost souls. "*

May 2, 1991

Mary: [Directions for Mary's statue in the Apparition Room] *"Please photograph this statue and put on it the title of 'Our Loving Mother.' Distribute it freely to My children. Let it be distributed far and wide. Many healings will be attributed to those who honor this picture. The picture is to be widely distributed everywhere as "Our Loving Mother." The image will bring with it many graces. Let there not be a single nation that does not have Heaven as the Loving Mother of God. Let there not be a single nation that does not have at least one of these cards with this image. I am honored in Heaven, but not so on earth. It is the Will of God that My Immaculate Heart will reign; and it is the Will of God that I be honored as your Loving Mother."*

May 9-10, 12, 1991

Jesus: *"The Holy Trinity of God is the greatest mystery of God. No greater mystery exists in all the universe. The Holy Trinity of God is the All Perfect, All Holy, undivided Unity. It is undivided because I am Love. Love is perfect, complete with no divisions. You do not divide the Love of God. You do not divide the Life of God. The mystery of the Holy Trinity cannot ever be fully comprehended by anyone. It is forever a revelation of God to all the angels, to all the saints, to all of creation. The mystery of the Holy Trinity is the core of God which no one, no creature, can ever fully comprehend. The greatness of God is beyond all creatures. Your life in Heaven is an ongoing revelation of God for eternity. "*

May 26, 1991

Jesus: *"This nation is heading toward a major war. Unless men turn back to me, I will not stop the punishment. Remember what My Mother told you: war is a punishment from God. People, if you do not want a punishment, turn back to Me without delay. I will echo the words of the Archangel Gabriel to you: 'The time is near.' "*

September 9, 1991

146

Jesus: *"My children have wandered very far from Me. They don't want to know Me and really don't care. Their hearts have grown cold and indifferent. Must I show them My might before they turn and come back to Me? The days are rapidly approaching when My punishment will begin. If man does not want My love and mercy, then man shall see My justice!"*

September 25, 1991

Jesus: *"Many of My children ask, but they don't get what they ask for because they do not keep My Commandments. Seek My Will and keep My Commandments; then you shall have what you ask for. Many of My children are deceived. They think they keep My Commandments but in fact they don't. My prideful children are like the Pharisees. Pride and love do not go hand in hand. Humility and love are joined."*

January 11, 1992

Jesus: *"A great punishment is coming for California. Do not fear speaking My words. There will be more hurricanes, more earthquakes, more tornadoes; more volcanoes will erupt and more violent storms will come, and great tidal waves will hit the shores of the earth!"*

August 31, 1992

Mary: *"My dear little children, time is running out. Time is My dear Son's gift to you. Please return this gift to My Son through prayer and the living of holy lives. Many of you are not prepared to greet My Son. Return to God without delay. You are stubborn and do not listen. More disasters will befall you. One will follow another quickly. By the grace of God, I am appearing in many places. I will end by saying that I invite you to be missionaries of My Son. I will depart, yet I will remain with you."*

August 31, 1992

Jesus added the following to the above the next day: *"Know that as the earth rumbles more and more, I am expressing My displeasure with the sins of mankind."*

147

Mary: *"The wrath of God is upon this nation and upon this world. Little children, I have come to you with tears for you are going to suffer. Permit Me to identify Myself again. I am the Immaculate Conception. I am the Spouse of the Holy Spirit. Behold a new Pentecost is coming. A new Heaven and a new earth is dawning, but first the old will be destroyed. Fire will fall down from Heaven, lightning will flash from one end of the sky to the other and the earth will plunge into a darkness it has never seen. The world has chosen these punishments. Fighting will increase among the nations, and there will be great unrest over the whole earth. Remain faithful to God and keep His Commandments in love. Show mercy to all and forgive as you forgiven. Pray, pray, pray; pray, pray, pray; pray, pray, pray. Tell the world I am mourning for the aborted children and for all lost souls. Your sacrifices and prayers can change the course of history. It is up to you."*

July 24, 1992

Jesus: *"The peace of the world has been entrusted to My Mother."*

Jesus: *"Bring the new ones, the old ones, the lost ones, the rebellious ones, the smart ones, the proud ones, the lame ones; bring them all for I am the One Who Heals!"*

(These last two quotes were undated)

* * * * * * * *

Nancy Fowler has been one of the principle messengers for Heaven's messages in the United States. Her counterpart in Ireland has been Christina Gallagher from County Mayo. Jesus and Mary have asked her to be Their instrument in calling back the Irish people to God's Commandments. Many of her messages appear in her book *Please Come Back To Me and My Son*, by R. Vincent. Many of them also pertain to the world at large as the subtitle indicates: *Our Lady's Appeal To The People Of Ireland and All Humanity*. The following are selected messages from the many which Christina has been receiving since 1988, which are still continuing and pertain to all the people of the world.

Mary: *"My child, tell all of My children to come back to Me and My Son. We are waiting for we love all of our children. Repent, go to Confession, unburden yourselves of all sin and then receive My Son's Body and Blood worthily. Pray and make sacrifices. In return, I will give you peace in your hearts. I love you all regardless of how far away you have strayed. My children, you have not much time until My Son's Hand will come over the earth in justice. Convert, I beg you, while you still have time. You do not know what God is going to send to mankind. My children who have come back to Me and My Son have nothing to fear."*

February 28, 1988

Mary: *"The people are not responding to My call. The smoke of Satan is rising from the earth. Look!"* [Here Christina sees in the sky a very large figure of Our Lord dressed in a white robe with his hand outstretched. He said: *""Woe!"* Balls of fire in great numbers were falling from the sky and as Christina looked, she could see people running in all directions, some falling, others huddled together. She did not see the fire strike anyone where it fell.]

March 1988

Mary: *"My child, the power of darkness overshadows My Church and the world. There are many of My children being lost, some forever. There are many who have made themselves slaves to My Heart. My child, the purification will come. Those who have served God in his light need not fear. Those of My children who will be lost forever cause Me great pain."*

July 23, 1988

Mary: *"Mankind has never indulged in Satan's work like now. My children must atone for sin. My son has broken the seal and drawn the sword."*

August 15, 1988

Mary: *"My child, the calamity has started. The influence of the Prince of Darkness is all around you. Arm yourself with My Rosary. My Church will be shaken, even to its very foundation. My children*

who want to be saved must repent. You are now like lambs among
wolves. Stand firm and have no fear, for the hand of the Mighty One
is with you. "

August 17, 1988

Mary: *"Always know that when you suffer pain, My dear Son is*
close by, and I, your Mother, the Mother of your Lord, am with you
as well. You are surrendering your body and soul to God. Keep your
heart with Jesus My Son and be always asking Him to save souls. My
Son will grant you what you ask in prayer. Many of My priests have
received the grace of pure conversion. Pure conversion means that
by the pure grace of God, they are converted in full. Pray now for the
gift of courage for them. "

September 24, 1988

Christina's visions of Hell and Purgatory: Jesus showed Christina
a vision of Hell which appeared as a great fire stretching into the
distance on every side with flames burning into flames with many
people, as it were, immersed in the fire through which she could see
them. The flames seemed to be going through the people and the scene
was very frightening. Jesus said to her: *"This is the abyss of sin, Hell,*
for all who do not love My Father. Do not be afraid of the world, but
work only for salvation. The purification is close at hand. Many will
be lost for the sins of the world and of the flesh. You must make
reparation for those whose eyes are blind and whose ears do not hear.
Pray and sacrifice for those who talk blasphemously about My son
on the See of Peter. "
When she first had her vision of Purgatory, she thought she was
in Hell, but she has since learned that there are different levels of
Purgatory. She has not seen the lowest level closest to Hell which is
called the Chambers of Suffering. She said: "One stage of it was as
if all was dead with no movement, only a constant longing to be
released, to be with God. Another time Jesus brought me as if under
a tunnel down steps into a dismal place. I could see a lot of people in
great distress. I could feel the sadness and suffering. Then I saw two
spirits whom I never realized could be in Purgatory: one a priest I
knew and another person." She felt a great depth of sorrow and
wanted both souls to be released. She then seemed to be pinned
against a wall with Jesus no longer there. The spirits were throwing
fire at her causing great pain, but she was resolved, if necessary, to

stay there so that these two persons she saw would be released. "As soon as I did this," she said, "an enormous ball of light came and surrounded me. I then found myself back in my home. I know for certain that these two souls were released."

March 29, 1989

Jesus: *"The three sins which grieve My Heart most deeply at this time are: abortion—the killing of the innocents; the sacrificing of the innocents to Satan; and the immoral abuse of the innocents."*

September 21, 1990

Father God: *"Tell all humanity to pray for the Spirit of Truth, the Spirit of Love. They are the One Spirit of Life Eternal. Many pray but live in the world and by the world. They adore all its fruits. Oh, but the day is coming faster than light when My mighty Hand will crush all the world. Today offer Me My Divine Son, through His wounds and sacrifice so that the world will prepare and make ready for the Second Coming of Jesus. As it stands now, they prepare for the coming of the Anti-Christ. Those who now live by the fruits of the world and worship thus, will receive of its fruits. They will drink of its bitter cup, and become followers of him-who-destroys. Tell all to prepare themselves. Make a place in their hearts only for Me, their Lord God who desires to save. The battle is on. Many souls are being lost. Go in peace."*

November 13, 1990

Jesus: *"Tell all humanity to prepare themselves. The time has come for the cleansing of all humanity. A great darkness will come upon the world. The heavens will shake. The only light will be through the Son of God and Man. The lightening bolts will flash like nothing the world has ever seen. My hand will come over the world more swiftly than the wind. The demons rage upon the earth. They are loosed from their pit. Tell all humanity of the Seven Seals. Pray, confess and seek only the Kingdom of God. My words will come to pass."* [Chapter 6 of Revelation opens with the words: "And I saw when the Lamb opened the first of the seven seals." The chapter closes with these fearsome words: "Fall on us and hide us from the Presence of the One who is seated on the throne, and from the wrath of the Lamb

151

for the great day of Their wrath has come and who is able to stand.")

November 13, 1990

Jesus: *"My people, I am Jesus, your Lord God. Many of you stand on the edge of the Abyss of Eternal Death. I say to you, My people, "Wake up!" My return to you is close at hand. My holy Mother calls you to prepare you for My coming. My holy Mother's calls have been unheard or scoffed at. My mercy will be with you now but for a short time more. My people, you are now living in the times of great darkness and distress. Wake up and be vigilant in prayer. My priest sons, if you do not fulfill My work on earth and proclaim My words in truth to all My people, you will force My Hand to fall on you in justice. I want My people to know My Word. I am Jesus, the Word, the Wisdom, the Truth and Eternal Life for you.*

April 23, 1991

Mary: *"The world is held by a pillar Who is Jesus Christ. The pillar is about to fall. My Divine Son, the Pillar of God, is soon releasing his hand. The world will be plunged into the depths of sin and drink of its bitterness. The clock, its alarm, is set. The hour is close. Pray, pray, pray."*

August 20, 1991

Christina: "The chastisement has to come to cleanse not only the world, but the Church as well because the darkness is even in the Church." She feels that the time is short, believing that everything she has been shown or told will be accomplished before the year 2000 is reached.

(undated)

* * * * * * * *

The following pages of messages from Heaven contain a wide selection from around the world, and they clearly are but a sampling of the thousands that have been given. They convincingly show us that Heaven is very serious indeed; that what it announces, it will

152

certainly do in the near future, even perhaps during this decade of the 1990s. They come from the four corners of the globe, indicating that Heaven is taking great pains to warn all people in every locale. They are rich and plentiful and echo the same call: repent for the time is short; return to God before His Hand is lowered. We are to assist everyone to wake up and prepare themselves so as not to lose their salvation. We begin with Mary's messages given at Fatima in 1917, for it is here that the great directions were set for this century. Mary gave Her messages to three children: Lucia, the oldest, and Jacinta and Francisco, brother and sister. Lucia still survives, living in a Carmelite convent in Spain.

Mary: *"I am the Lady of the Rosary. I have come to warn the faithful to amend their lives and to ask pardon for their sins. They must not offend Our Lord anymore, for He is already offended by men's sins. People must say the Rosary. Let them continue to say it everyday. "*

Mary: *"I have come to ask for the consecration of Russia to My Immaculate Heart and the Communion of reparation on the first Saturdays of each month. If people listen to My requests, Russia will be converted and the world will have peace. If not, Russia will scatter her errors throughout the world provoking wars and persecutions of the Church. The good will be martyred, the Holy Father will have much to suffer, and various nations will be destroyed. But in the end, My Immaculate Heart will triumph. The Holy Father will consecrate Russia to me; it will be converted and a certain period of peace will be given to the world. . .When you say the Rosary say after each Mystery: 'O My Jesus, forgive us our sins, save us from the fires of Hell, and lead all souls to Heaven, especially those most in need of Thy mercy.'"*

* * * * * * * *

To Sister Faustina, Polish nun and mystic who received the stigmata and who was chosen to reveal to the world God's Divine Mercy being expended upon the world in these latter times. She died at 33 years of age and wrote her diary in the 1930s.

Jesus: *"Let the greatest sinners place their trust in My mercy. They have the right before others to trust in the abyss of My mercy. Write about My great mercy given for tormented souls. Souls that make an appeal to My mercy delight Me very much. To such souls I grant even more graces than they ask. I cannot punish even the* *greatest sinner if he makes an appeal to My compassion; but on the contrary, I justify him in unfathomable and inscrutable mercy. Write to them: I come as a Just Judge, but first I open wide the door of My mercy.* "

Mary: "*I gave the Savior to the world. As for you, you have to speak to the world about His great mercy and prepare the world for the Second Coming of Him Who will come, not as a merciful Savior, but as a Just Judge. Oh, how terrible is that day. Determined is the Day of Justice, the Day of Divine Wrath. The angels tremble before it. Speak to souls about this great mercy while there is still time for granting mercy.* "

Sr. Faustina: "All light in the heavens will be extinguished and there will be a great darkness over the entire earth. Then the sign of the Cross will be seen in the sky, and from the openings where the hands and feet of the Savior were nailed, will come forth great lights which will lighten up the earth for a period of time. This will take place shortly before the last day."

* * * * * * * *

The following LIFE OFFERING with its accompanying promises were given to a hidden contemplative nun in Hungary. It is not well known in the West as it has only been received and translated a short time ago. Many supernatural events and messages were given to special souls in the Eastern Bloc countries through many years of communistic oppression, but were kept hidden because of their persecution of religion. These messages with their beautiful promises were given in 1955. Sister has wished to keep her anonymity.

Mary implores those who receive Holy Communion daily or at least weekly to offer their lives for the greater glory of God and the salvation of souls, so that the souls of sinners may not be damned, but instead to receive at least in their last hour the graces of eternal life. She has promised to those who make the LIFE OFFERING TO JESUS below the following five great promises:

1. Their names will be written in the Hearts of Jesus and Mary inflamed by love.

2. Their Life Offering, together with the infinite merits of

Jesus, can save many souls from damnation. All souls who will live until the end of the world will benefit from their Life Offering they make.

3. None of their family members will go to Hell, even if it would seem otherwise from their lifestyles because they will receive in the depth of their souls the grace of sincere contrition before the soul departs from their body.

4. On the day they offer their lives to Jesus, their loved ones suffering in Purgatory will be released.

5. She will be with them at the hour of their death. They will not know Purgatory. Mary will carry their souls straight to the Presence of the glorious Trinity, where they will live with Her in a special place created by God and will rejoice forever.

TEXT OF THE LIFE OFFERING TO JESUS

My dear Jesus, before the Holy Trinity, our Heavenly Mother, and the whole Heavenly Court, united with Your most Precious Blood and Your Sacrifice on Calvary, I hereby offer my whole life to the intention of Your Sacred Heart and to the Immaculate Heart of Mary. Together with my life I place at Your disposal all Holy Masses, all my Holy Communions, all my good deeds, all my sacrifices, and the sufferings of my entire life for the adoration and supplication of the Holy Trinity, for unity in our Holy Mother Church, for the Holy Father, for bishops and priests, for good priestly vocations, and for all souls until the end of the world. O my Jesus, please accept my life sacrifice and my offerings; give me Your grace that I may persevere obediently until my death. Amen.

NOTE: This Life Offering should be made with a humble heart, a firm resolve and with a pure intention. Make this Life Offering only when you feel ready to do so and when you will stand by it. It should be renewed from time to time.

Mary adds the following motherly advice for this Offering: *"My children who offer their lives, make an Act of Contrition every day! Make it not only for yourselves, but include all people. This will continually weaken the power of evil to tempt and it will help all souls to free themselves from the slavery of sin. See how great the power of sincere contrition can be when it comes from the depths of the heart. It can heal, cleanse and save the life of the soul. In addition to your* *frequent Contrition made for all humanity, unite yourselves with My Immaculate Heart in order to storm Heaven with prayer for the forgiveness of sins. Thus you will become united with Me and become genuine and intimate helpers of Jesus as fishers of men. "*

Mary appeared to a forester named Matous Lasuta from June 1 to August 9, 1958, in the northern mountains of Turzovka, Czechoslovakia, in a remarkable series of seven apparitions and accompanying visions of God's future punishments on the world. The shrine is now as famous for the Eastern European countries as Lourdes has been for Western Europe.

On July 1st, the Blessed Virgin showed Lasuta how the chastisement could be avoided or made lighter through prayer, saying the Rosary and penance. Prayer can hold off the justice of God. Such prayer must come from the heart; it must not just come from the mind or intellect or be said absentmindedly. Good works must be accomplished as well. Each of the apparitions were graphic descriptions of the pending punishments to come. For example, one of his visions was described by Matous as follows: "Powerful explosions burst forth suddenly over the water and land. A dense rain of small leaves fell on the earth. As the leaves reached the ground, they burst into flames. Soon all of the soil touched by the leaves was covered with fire." He saw particular countries on which they fell, but he was forbidden to divulge their names. Mary told him: *"Matous, what you have seen, make known to the world. "* What he was to tell the world included:

1. God's punishment will strike out about two-thirds of all humanity.
2. The sun will cease to give its warmth; there will be cold summers with poor harvests.
3. There will be terrible floods and other misfortunes caused through natural elements.
4. There will be numerous earthquakes that will move mountains.
5. Churches, houses and buildings will move off their foundations and be carried away by floods.
6. Nonbelievers will blaspheme God in their despair.
7. The air will be filled with visible demon-like forms which will represent sins and vices. These phantoms will terrify humanity.

After this, nature will calm down again and a bright light will appear. The world will seem unrecognizable, for everything will have been destroyed. It will be difficult to find life and living human beings. God will punish the wicked and all those who have blasphemed Him.

For those chosen good souls during this nightmare of horror, Mary gives these words of comfort and direction:

Mary: *"All My children will receive and carry the sign of the Cross on their foreheads. My chosen ones alone will see this sign. These chosen ones will be instructed by My angels as how to conduct themselves. My faithful will be without any kind of fear during the most difficult hours. They will be protected by the good spirits and will be fed by Heaven. From them they will receive further instructions. They will fall into a death-like sleep while being continually protected by the angels. When they awaken, they will be like newly born. Their bodies will be beautiful and their souls will be steeped in God. Everything they do will be for the glory of God. The earth will be beautiful again and My chosen ones will see how God takes care of them. "*

Mary: *"Love Me more from day to day! The more you love God and the more you love Me, all the more courageous you will be during these days of fear. These times will start with freezing nights, rolling thunder and the trembling of the earth. Pray and cross yourselves frequently with the sign of the Cross, repent of your sins and call upon the Mother of God for help for She will take you under Her protection. "*

Mary: *"The angels who are entrusted with the work of destruction are ready, but the wrath of God can be stayed by praying the Rosary, by penance and sacrifices of the sinner's repentance. "*

* * * * * * * *

Elizabeth Szanto-Kindelmann lived all her life in Hungary, from 1913 to April 11, 1985. She was widowed early in life with six children to raise alone. Her mission from Heaven was to give to the world messages relating to Mary's Immaculate Heart centered on a devotion called FLAME OF LOVE. They are recorded in a book of the same title. Just a few of the many rich and beautiful revelations concerning Mary's Immaculate Heart are given here.

Mary: *"My daughter, I ask you to hold Thursdays and Fridays as days of special graces. Regard them as days of Reparation and Atonement to My Divine Son. The way to achieve this is with a Family Holy Hour. During this hour of prayer, you should recite various* *prayers such as the Rosary and sing hymns. Begin your worship by making the sign of the Cross five times in honor of My Son's five wounds. Finish the hour with five Crosses as well. Continue your worship with Scriptural and spiritual readings. Also light a candle in remembrance of My promise. Try to hold these prayer sessions in groups of two or three persons at least, because where two or three gather in the name of the Lord, My Son Jesus will be there. The flame of grace which I give you from My Immaculate Heart must go from heart to heart. It will be the miracle by which you will bind Satan. It is the fire of love and unity; and with it we shall extinguish fire with fire—the fire of hatred with the fire of love. I wish that the Flame of Love of My Immaculate Heart will be known everywhere just as My name is known over all the world. I will blind Satan with the flame of My Heart. My Heart's Flame of Love will burn up all sin!"*

April 13, 1962

Mary: *"Do you know My daughter that these Thursday and Friday times of prayer with the family are special days of great graces? In the hours of prayer and reparation, the power of Satan will decrease in proportion to the fervor with which people will pray for sinners."*

September 18, 1962

Mary: *"My daughter, your compassion for suffering souls moves My motherly heart so much that I will grant the grace that if anyone anywhere will say three Hail Marys in remembrance of My Flame of Love, on each occasion a soul will be freed from Purgatory. Furthermore, during November, the month of the Holy Souls, ten souls will be freed from Purgatory for each Hail Mary fervently prayed. Suffering souls will also feel the effect of the graces coming from My motherly heart's Flame of Love."*

Jesus: *"My teachings are simple and childlike. Heaven belongs to childlike souls which never ponder. It belongs to those who listen to Me in wonder and believe in me. Behold, I do not speak to you in the language of science. Science has never made anyone holy yet! Accept My simple teachings implanted in your childlike souls. Behold, My Kingdom belongs to them."*

May 19, 1963

Mary: *"I save mankind from the sinful smoky lava of hate. Not one dying person's soul should go to Hell. My flame of love is beginning to light. Chosen souls have to fight the Prince of Darkness. It will be a terrible storm, like a hurricane devastating everything. What is so terrible is that Satan wishes to destroy the faith and trust of My chosen ones. I will be with you everywhere in the approaching storm, for I am your Mother. I can and will help you!"*

May 19, 1963

Mary: *"I extend My Heart's Flame of Love to all peoples and nations on earth, not only to those who dwell in the Catholic Church, but to all those in the world who are marked with the sign of the Holy Cross of My Divine Son. The Flame of Love which I wish to spread over you more and more will have an effect on the suffering souls in Purgatory as well. Those families who keep the Holy Hour of Reconciliation on Thursday or Fridays will receive special graces through which they can liberate a member of their family from Purgatory by keeping only one strict day of fast on bread and water."*

September 12-16, 1963

Jesus: *"Your soul which lives in the mud of the earth cannot free itself. I have to take you out of it; then I have to wash you with My Precious Blood. Prostrate yourself before My Holy Cross and the Precious Blood will fall on you. The drops of My Blood are like a blank check in your hands. Anyone can cash it before his death. But you never know the hour of your death, so do not delay in cashing it before your old age!"*

Jesus to mothers/parents: *"To all you mothers who bring pleasure to My Heart, I say that the merits of your work are no less than the work of a priest in high office. You parents, you mothers, understand the sublime vocation which I have entrusted to you. You are destined to populate My Kingdom. From your hearts, from your bosoms come forth every step My Church takes. My Kingdom grows according to how you mothers take care of My created souls. You have the greatest and above all the most responsible task. This task I placed in your hands to lead multitudes of souls to salvation. To this, your responsible tasks, I give My special blessing."*

February 29, 1964

Jesus: *"Before the coming difficult times befall you, prepare yourself for the vocation I have called each of you to. Do not live in indifference and idleness. The approaching storm will carry away the idle and indifferent souls. Only those souls who are able to make sacrifices will be saved. The storm will start when I lift My Hand. Give My warning to everyone, especially to priests. Let My warning shake you from your indifference in advance. "*

March 12, 1964

Jesus: *"Your constant humble repentance is the shortest way to me. By this you attract Me and so does every soul who repents. I ask all of you, please attract Me to yourselves. This is the most perfect tool in your hand to oblige Me; then I cannot refuse anything you ask Me. I shower you with the abundance of My graces for your humble repentance. Do you know what makes Me love you? Your sincere contrition. This makes Me intoxicated. Do you see, little soul, of what great things you are capable? Comprehend this great miracle that you can make Me happy with your sincere repentance. "*

July 26-27, 1964

Jesus: *"Those meek souls who try to avoid making sacrifices. Their inaction hurts My Heart when I glance at the multitude of timid souls who live a good life but avoid making sacrifices. They think that a good life alone will merit them eternal life. They repent of their sins but not for the love of Me. Tell them that without sacrifice, there is no spiritual progress. It is a misconception that I am satisfied with barren goodness. It is like the tree which did not bring forth fruit in the Gospels. Such souls do not even think about how gray and dull they are. The light of My graces will illuminate only those souls who are aflame with love. This light will be in proportion to how much they allow My graces to work within them to form them. "*

November 8, 1964

* * * * * * * *

Sister Agnes Sasagawa Katsuko was born in 1931. She entered the convent of the Servants of the Eucharist at Akita, Japan, 200 kilometers north of Tokyo. From 1973 to 1981 she was the recipient of many heavenly messages and events. From January 4, 1975, to September 15, 1981, a statue of the Virgin Mary wept human tears 101 times; sometimes even blood came forth from the eyes of the statue. From this far corner of the globe, God again emphasizes the coming chastisement upon the world; these apparitions have been approved by the local ordinary, Bishop John Shojiro Ito, of the Diocese of Niigata on April 22, 1984.

Mary: *"Many men in this world afflict the Lord. I desire souls to console Him in order to soften the anger of the Heavenly Father. I wish with My son for souls who will by their suffering and poverty enact reparation for the many sinners and ungrateful ones. In order to show His anger, the Heavenly Father is preparing to inflict a heavy chastisement on all humanity. I have intervened several times to appease the wrath of the Father. I have been able to withhold calamities by offering Him the sufferings of His Son on the Cross, His Precious Blood and those beloved souls who console Him, who form the cohort of victim souls. Prayer, penance and courageous sacrifice may soften the Father's anger; I ask this also of your community. "*

August 3, 1973

Mary: *"As I have already told you, if men do not repent and better themselves, Father God will inflict a terrible punishment on all humanity. It will be a punishment greater than the Deluge, such as one that has never been seen before. Fire will fall from the sky and will wipe out a great part of humanity, the good as well as the bad, sparing neither priests nor the faithful. The survivors will find themselves so desolate that they will envy the dead. The only weapons which will remain for you will be the Rosary and the sign left by My Son. Each day recite the prayers of the Rosary. With the Rosary pray for the Pope, such a way that one will see cardinals opposing cardinals, bishops against other bishops. The priests who venerate Me will be scorned and opposed by their confreres. Churches and altars will be sacked. The Church will be full of those who make compromises, and demons will press many priests and consecrated souls to leave the service of the Lord. The demons will be especially implacable against souls consecrated to God. I alone am able to save you from the calamities which approach. Those who place their confidence in Me will be saved. "*

October 13, 1973

* * * * * * * *

Oierina Gilli, from the towns of Montichiari-Fontanelle, Italy, was chosen by Mary to make known Mary as the *Rosa Mystica* or Mystical Rose. Her appearances to her began in 1947 and continued on through many years. This devotion to Mary under this title steadily increased in popularity and numbers around the world through the multiplying of statues of Mary depicted as the Mystical Rose. Two important messages are given here:

Mary: *"The times are getting worse and worse. A terrible danger is threatening. The Church too is in great danger. Things will get so bad that people will think all is lost. As you can observe for yourself, human pride has resulted in confusing those in the highest offices of the Church. They wish to drive Me the Mother out of the Holy Church and tear Me from My children's hearts."*

January 30, 1975

Mary: *"For hundreds of years I have come down to many places throughout the world time and time again. If since My assumption into Heaven I had not returned frequently to earth to gather My children around me, the world would have grown to a great extent cold and dry to the Lord without My motherly and loving intervention."*

1976
(specific date not recorded)

* * * * * * * *

To Italian mystic and stigmatist, Elena Leonardi:

Mary: *"The earth will tremble in a most frightful way and all humanity will stagger. An unforeseen fire will descend over the whole earth and a great part of humanity will be destroyed."*

April 1, 1976

Mary: *"The world is at the edge of a precipice. Society is at the point of terrible punishments. There will be many dead, there will be sicknesses, there will be great wars. God will permit Satan to sow division between governments, societies and families. There will be much physical and moral suffering. God will abandon all of them and send them untold punishments. The punishments which are near are very horrible. "*

December 11, 1981

* * * * * * * *

To Spanish stigmatist Amparo Cuevos, Escorial, Spain:

Mary: *"My daughter and all My dear children. Be alert. Satan wants to take hope away from you! He knows very well that if he succeeds in this, he will take everything from you. A soul which loses hope is ready to commit sin. Without hope, man is in deep darkness. He no longer sees with the eyes of faith and for him all virtue and goodness lose their value. "*

December 12, 1981

* * * * * * * *

Surely some of the most famous apparitions of modern times are those to the six children of Medjugorje, Yugoslavia. They have been occurring daily since June 24, 1981, now more than eleven years. Literally more than a thousand messages have been given by Mary, and scores of books and magazines have been promoting Her words and instructions. It has been a village where faith has been redis-covered for millions. Mary's messages there have not been as strong-ly apocalyptical as others which are presented, but by the very fact of Her intense and loving care for the world shown there, we know that they portent a climax in our human history. Medjugorje's mes-sage is one of commitment to God, fasting, faith, peace, and prayer. The following are a few of the many, many messages given by Mary there:

Mary: *"It is necessary to tell everyone that from the very beginning of My coming here, I have been conveying the message of God to the world. It is a great pity not to believe in My coming. Faith is a vital element, but one cannot compel a person to believe. Faith is the foundation from which everything flows."*

December 11, 1981

Mary: *"The best fast is on bread and water. Through fasting and prayer, one can stop wars, one can suspend the laws of nature. Charity cannot replace fasting. Those who are not able to fast, can find something else to replace it with, such as prayer, doing good deeds, giving alms; but everyone should fast except the sick."*

July 21, 1982

Mary: *"One goes to Heaven in full conscience: that which you have now. At the moment of death, you are conscious of the separation of the body and soul. It is false to teach people that you are reborn many times and that you pass into different bodies. One is born only once. The body drawn from the earth decomposes after death. It never comes back to life again. Man receives a transfigured body."*

July 24, 1982

Mary: *"Whoever has done very much evil during this life can go straight to Heaven if he confesses, is very sorry for what he had done and receives Communion at the end of his life."*

July 24, 1982

Mary: *"Today many persons go to Hell. God allows His children to suffer in Hell due to the fact that they have committed grave, unpardonable sins. Those who are in Hell no longer have a chance to know a better lot."*

July 25, 1982

Mary: *"In Purgatory there are different levels; the lowest is close to Hell and the highest gradually draws near to Heaven. It is not on All Souls Day but at Christmas that the greatest number of souls leave*

Purgatory. There are in Purgatory souls who pray ardently to God, but for whom no relative or friend prays on earth. God makes them benefit from the prayers of other people. It happens that God permits them to manifest themselves in different ways, close to their relatives on earth, in order to remind men of the existence of Purgatory and to solicit their prayers to come close to God Who is just, but good. The majority of people go to Purgatory. Many go to Hell. A small number go directly to Heaven. "

January 10, 1983

Mary: *"You cannot imagine what is going to happen nor what the Eternal Father will send to earth. That is why you must be converted! Renounce everything. Do penance. Express My thanks to all My children who have prayed and fasted. I carry all this to My Divine Son in order to obtain an alleviation of His justice against the sins of mankind. "*

June 24, 1983

Mary: *"Begin by calling the Holy Spirit each day. The most important thing is to pray to the Holy Spirit. When the Holy Spirit descends on earth, then everything becomes clear and everything is transformed. "*

October 21, 1983

Mary: "The Mass is the greatest prayer of God. You will never be able to understand its greatness. That is why you must be perfect and humble at Mass, and you should prepare yourselves there."

December 26, 1983

Vicka, one of the visionaries from Medjugorje, describes her vision of Hell: "We could see people before they went into the fire and then saw them coming out of the fire. Before they went into the fire they looked like normal people. The more they are against God's Will, the deeper they went into the fire; and the deeper they go in, the more they rage against Him. When they come out of the fire, they no longer have human shape anymore; instead they are more like grotesque animals unlike anything here on earth. These were people who denied and hated God. They went into the fire naked and emerged with horrible blackened skin. Mary said to us: *"People will tear their hair, brothers will plead with brothers, they will curse their past lives without God. They will repent but then it will be too late."*

NOTE: The Virgin Mary told seer Maria Pavlovic on November 30, 1983, to have her pastor and spiritual director at the time, Franciscan Father Tomislav Vlasic, to write to the Holy Father about her apparitions at Medjugorje. He did so with a fine overview of the tremendous series of apparitions and heavenly manifestations that had been occurring in their village since 1981. Herein are some segments of Fr. Thomas's letter to Pope John Paul II:

All the seers declare in substance that they see the Blessed Virgin as they see other people. They speak with Her and touch Her. The Blessed Virgin told them: *"Peace in the world is in a state of crisis."* She continually invites everyone to reconciliation and conversion. She promised that She would leave a visible sign at the place of the apparition of Medjugorje for all humanity to witness. The time preceding this visible sign is a period of grace for conversion and a deepening of faith. The Blessed Mother promised to confide secrets to the children.

Mary gave to Mirjana a special message on December 25, 1982. In summary it said: *"Before the visible sign is given to humanity, three warnings will be given to the world. The warnings are events on the earth. Mirjana will be a witness to them. After the admonition, the visible sign will take place where apparitions appear in Medjugorje for all humanity."*

The ninth and tenth secrets are grave. They are a chastisement for the sins of the world. The punishment is inevitable because we must not expect a conversion of the entire world. The chastisement can be decreased by prayers and penance, but it cannot be suppressed. After the first admonition, the other will follow in a rather brief period of time. In this way, mankind will have time for conversion. This time, this period of grace is urgent. After the visible sign, those still living will have little time for conversion. For that reason, the Blessed Virgin invites us to urgent reconciliation and conversion now.

In 1982 Mirjana related to me another apparition in which Satan came transformed as the Blessed Virgin. He asked Mirjana to renounce the Madonna and follow him so that she would be happy in love and life. With the Virgin she would have only to suffer. She repulsed him. Immediately the Blessed Virgin arrived and Satan disappeared. Then Mary gave her these most important words.

Mary: *"Please excuse Me for this, but you must know that*

Satan exists. One day he presented himself before the throne of God and requested permission to put the Church of God on trial during a period of one century. This century is under the powers of the Devil, but when these secrets which are being confided to you are realized, his power will be destroyed. He has already begun to lose his power and he has become aggressive. He destroys marriages, creates division between priests, and causes obsessions and murders. You should protect yourself from these things by fasting and prayer. Especially by community prayer. Carry blessed objects with you and keep them in your houses. Come back to the custom of using Holy Water. "

* * * * * * * *

Mary spoke to stigmatist Mryna (Maria Al Akhras) Nazzours of Damascus, Syria. Incredibly, healing olive oil exudes from both Mryna's hands and face, as well as from hundreds of icons of Mary. This phenomenon, unique in all of history, began in 1982 and still continues.

Mary: *"My children, be mindful of God. God is with us. You know a great deal, but you know nothing. Your knowledge is incomplete. The day will come when you will know all things as God knows Me. Deal kindly with those who do you wrong; do not mistreat anyone. I have given you oil, more than you have asked for. I will give you something stronger than oil. Repent and believe. Preach My Son, Emmanuel. Those who preach Him are saved. Those who do not preach Him are false believers. I do not ask you to give money to the churches; what I ask for you is love. Those who give money to the poor and to the churches and yet have no love are worthless. "*

1982
(specific date not recorded)

* * * * * * * *

Joseph Terelya was the son of militant Communist officials in his native Ukraine, a part of the U.S.S.R. He was secretly baptized by his grandmother. From his teens he lived a very militant Christian existence, defending his faith by spending twenty-three years in

Communist prisons, often to the point of death. Twice he was revived from certain death by the appearances of the Blessed Virgin and St. Michael. Expelled from the Ukraine in 1987, he now resides as a stateless person in Canada. His story is told in the gripping and stirring book of his experiences in prison under the communists: *Witness: Joseph Terelya, Apparitions and Persecutions In the USSR.*

Mary: *"Lucifer is losing strength. To maintain himself on the throne of darkness, he began portraying himself as repentant, but this is not true. Lucifer is cunning and clever. He is preparing a great deception for all of God's creation, and especially for the people of God. For a short time a godless kingdom shall maintain itself from one end of the earth to the other. "*

(undated)

St. Michael: *"How many warnings must mankind be given before it repents? The world continues on the road of self-will and hedonism. The world would long ago have been destroyed but the world's soul would not allow this. As the soul preserves the life of the body, so do Christians preserve the life of the world. God needs fervent and constant sons. You shall go through the ways of the world and give witness. In the end, God will punish the apostates because only through this punishment will God be able to bring mankind back to sound reason. Satan will begin a new persecution for the Christians. Times of persecution will begin for both the priests and the faithful. The world will be divided into the messengers of God and the messengers of Anti-Christ. After the great revelations of the Virgin Mary, renewal of love for Christ will begin. "*

July 17, 1983

* * * * * * * *

Oliveto Citra, like many Italian villages, is built on a hilltop. It is located two hours from Naples in a south-easterly direction. On the evening of May 24, 1985, about a dozen children were surprised by a vision of Mary. This began ongoing visions in this remote area of southern Italy which continue today. More than fifty persons have now seen the Madonna at various times singly and in groups. One of these was Mafalda Mattia. This is the message Mary left with her.

168

Mary: *"The world is on the edge of a yawning precipice; pray, pray particularly for the heads of the great nations because they have no time to pray being so preoccupied with preparing for war and spreading violence. My dear children, God has sent Me to earth to save all of you because the entire world is in danger. I came into your midst to bring peace to your hearts. He wants peace to reign in the hearts of all and desires the conversion of all. My dear children, pray, pray, pray for this intention. If you do not pray, you will not receive anything. The time at your disposal is short. There will be earthquakes and great misfortunes and even famine for all the inhabitants of the earth. My dear children, when God comes among you He does not come for mere amusement. Nor is He afraid of the powerful or the indifferent. So take this message seriously. I will ask God not to punish you. God says to all: Save yourselves, pray a great deal and do penance. Humanity is replete with serious sins that are an offense to the love of God. Peace on earth is about to end. The world cannot be saved without peace; men will only find peace if they return to God."*

(undated)

* * * * * * * *

Additional later messages given to the Hidden Nun of Hungary:

Mary: *"My children, if you patiently carry the little thorn from the Cross of My Son that He has given you, you can save countless souls from eternal damnation. Thus holding the hand of your Heavenly Mother, you too will partake in the work of redemption. My children, do not ask for sufferings, but always accept with humility and selflessness those which the Lord hands to you. My Holy Son finished the work of redemption. His own sacrifice was enough; however, He left a little part for each of you. To participate in the work of redemption means much sacrifice."*

(undated)

Mary: *"My children, all men, whether they are in the state of grace or are fallen sinners, are the children of your Heavenly Mother and are brothers and sisters of My Holy Son until the moment when the Gates of Hell close behind an unfortunate soul. Brothers and sisters are responsible for each other. At the Last Judgment, the Lord will ask each and everyone: 'What have you done for your fellow* *human beings while you were on earth? Did you mitigate their sufferings? Did you console them that they might carry the cross of life a little easier? What kind of sacrifice did you make to help at least one human being to gain eternal life?'"*

September 24, 1986

* * * * * * * *

Another remarkable visionary and mystic is Mrs. Gladys Quiroga de Motta from San Nicolos, Argentina. She received apparitions and messages from Mary from September 24, 1983, to February, 1990. Since then, Our Lady continues to appear to her, but without messages for the world. In Argentina, the response to the apparitions has been overwhelming. On the 25th of each month, more than 50,000 pilgrims hold a procession from the Cathedral to the site of the apparitions. The Bishop, Msgr. Castagna, is very supportive of the devotions and the reality of the visits of Mary. Progress is being made toward an official recognition; a new basilica sanctuary will be constructed on the apparition site.

Mary: *"He who listens to My words will find salvation. He who puts them into practice will live forever. Those who hope in God do not hope in vain. "*

June 15, 1984

Jesus: *"If this generation does not listen to My Mother, it will perish. I ask everyone to listen to Her. Man's conversion is necessary. It is better to look up and to know what He who is there says, rather than be adrift spiritually. Think about it! "*

March 12, 1986

Jesus: *"Youth rushes sadly to perdition along the easy road of drugs. This is the panorama which the Evil One spreads in front of them; a whole range of sins separates them more and more from God. All that is required is that they look to the Mother of God, their Mother, and She will lead them to God. They must enter into the mind of Mary in order to hear the voice of God. I do not hide Myself. No* *one should avoid Me. Amen. (Read Luke 12: 29-32.)"*

September 21, 1987

Jesus: *"I warn the world today for it is not aware that souls are in danger. Many are lost. Few will find salvation unless they accept Me as their Savior. My mother must be accepted. My Mother must be heard in the totality of Her messages. The world must discover the richness which She brings to Christians. The children of sin will grow up in sin if their unbelief increases. I want a renewal of the spirit, a detachment from death and an attachment to life. I have chosen the Heart of My Mother so that what I ask for will be achieved. Souls will come to Me through the means of Her Immaculate Heart.*

November 19, 1987

Jesus: *"Mankind is in the process of falling into a progressive self-destruction. That is why it is necessary now to disseminate the words of the Mother. The Lord has marked this time with a sign: the Woman clothed with the sun (Rev. 12:1). She represents the hope to which Her children must cling. The Mother has looked on you. It is up to you to set your eyes of your heart on God."*

February 28, 1989

Jesus: *"In the ancient past, the world was saved by the Ark of Noah. Today My Mother is the Ark. It is through Her that souls will be saved because She will lead them to Me. He who rejects My Mother rejects Me. Many are those who allow the grace of God to pass these days."*

December 30, 1989

NOTE: Mary gave Gladys more than 1,800 messages from 1983 to 1990; Jesus gave her 68.

* * * * * * * *

In 1987 Mary began a series of remarkable appearances to crowds of people in the village of Hrushiv, Ukraine. These lasted for several months and were seen by more than 300,000 people during this period. During these apparitions many received individual messages from Mary as they applied to the person. Josyp Terelya, recently released from prison, was welcomed by the crowds of people and was acknowledged by them as one of their Church leaders. Mary gave the people these messages through him at two different occasions then:

Mary: *"Pray the Rosary, pray the Hail Mary with devotion and with living faith. Satan loses his power during the prayer of the Our Fathers. I beseech you insistently to teach your children to pray the Rosary. The Rosary is a most powerful weapon against Satan for a devout person to use. Carry your Rosary with you always. Whoever wants to receive grace from God should pray constantly and take upon himself voluntary penances. Be merciful. Remember that the Rosary will preserve mankind from sin and perdition. Even carry it around your necks and avail yourselves of it when in need. Pray for ravaged Russia; you will save the world by your prayers.*

"Teach children to pray. Teach children to live in truth and live yourselves in this same truth. Forgive nations that have harmed you. Constantly say the Rosary, for it is a weapon against Satan. He fears the Rosary. Say it everyday, frequently at any gathering of people. Repent and love one another. The times are coming which have been foretold as being those of the end of times. See the desolation which surrounds the world. See the sins of sloth and genocide. I come to you with tears in My eyes and I implore you to pray and work for good and for the glory of God. Ukraine was the first country to acknowledge Me as Queen and so I have received her under My care. Work for God, for without this there is no happiness and no one will enter the Kingdom of God."

1987
(specific date not recorded)

* * * * * * * *

On the other side of the globe, Mary again visited the Orient, coming to a young newly converted housewife named Julia Kim. Korea unfortunately has very many abortions, one of the highest per capita in the world. The Virgin Mary addressed this sad situation in a most singular and dramatic way. On numerous occasions, Julia was to suffer the actual pains which a fetus in the womb would suffer when being aborted. Mary's appearances began first with a weeping statue of Mary which continued to weep from June 19, 1985, onward. Sometimes the statue would weep blood! The following account takes place at Naju in 1988:

Mary addressed Julia Kim regarding the vast numbers of abortions that are committed daily around the world: *"Thank you, My daughter. Could you suffer more for Me? Because of your sufferings endured today, 5,000 souls have converted and have been offered to God. It is necessary to make this known to many souls. In recalling the children they have rejected in their wombs by abortion, many souls received the grace of conversion. Many souls walk miserably on the road to Hell not knowing that they are murderers killing without any pity. After having deprived these defenseless ones of their human dignity, what suffering could be more atrocious than that of these little lives forced to undergo monstrous cruelty which actually belongs to the parents themselves? These are little lives without sin. I cannot but be sad in the face of such ignorance and indifference on the part of parents who have come to the point of killing sacred lives which God has given to them by crushing them brutally beneath their feet, cruelly tearing them out of their wombs. That is why, by showing you the reality of these 'little lives' who implore and beg to be let to live, I desire that many sinners make penance and return to Me. I beg you to make it known to all that from the moment a little life is formed in the womb of a mother, it is not a mere clot of blood but a human being in whom there is life and soul. "*

1988
(specific date not recorded)

* * * * * * * *

Mary appeared to Patricia Talbott of El Cajas, Ecuador, a youthful visionary who first encountered the Virgin Mary on August 28, 1988. She was only sixteen years old at the time. Mary continued the apparitions and messages for eighteen months. The following are some of the most important ones that again address the impending difficulties facing all of mankind:

Mary: *"The Rosary is the most complete prayer. Do not ask yourselves why you pray it. Let it be your shield against the Evil One* *who is acting. Do not detach yourselves from it. The Spirit of God descends upon you. You have the great mission of the conversion of the world. Please, little children, make evil disappear. It is in your hands that the Hand of My Son be detained or that you suffer as strongly as the sorrow of His Heart."*

December 25, 1988

Mary: *"I am your Mother, remain in constant prayer. Earthquakes will come, hurricanes and the sky will shower fire, for all this will come from the Father, the Son and the Spirit of God. In those days men will be destroyed because of their lukewarmness. You yourselves will create your own destruction. You do not know the sorrow I feel as I announce these natural catastrophes and those created by men. You are only a step away now. Do not allow this to happen. Recite more prayers and pray the Rosary as a family. Go to Mass frequently. I love you so much, My children, and I am the guardian of your faith. He who is with God will be protected under My mantle, in the Heart of My Son and in My Heart."*

January 1, 1989

Mary: *"Today is the day of My physical departure but My spiritual retreat will never be, for I will be with you always. I ask you for prayer, fasting and penance. Children, in the end God will triumph over all things. Remember the first Commandment to love one another and to love God above all things. Children, priests and religious, help in the conversion of the world, the redemption of souls and the purification. Young people, be examples of light. The sick are indeed chosen by God, chosen for the redemption of the world. At the end of all the apparitions in the world, I will leave a great sign in those places where I have been. Goodbye, My little ones."*

February 3, 1990

* * * * * * * *

To Julka of Yugoslavia, widow and mother of two children, was given a vision of the coming punishment:

Julka: "The chastisement will begin with a strong warm wind along with ten claps of thunder that will strike with such a force that it will shudder throughout the world. It will be like a terrific hurricane accompanied with a series of earthquakes with the sky alight with fire. The whole atmosphere of the earth from ground to sky will be a gigantic sheet of flame. After this, the sun will turn red as blood followed by a creeping darkness rising up like a mist. In that darkness Jesus will appear in a bright yellow light surrounded with white clouds." [Note: Julka was given this graphic vision of the coming chastisement. Jesus later said to her of this: *"As you have seen, so will it be. I shall come quickly and in splendor. All of My creatures who survive the Great Tribulation will see Me. "*

(undated)

* * * * * * * *

Zdenko Jim Singer, Croatian-born Canadian, had amazing apparitions and messages from Jesus for 99 continuous days which began on May 28, 1989. Once again, a gifted soul helps to reveal more of the mystical puzzle of our pending future which is unfolding around us in these times. Satan is referred to as the Shining Darkness in these visions:

Jesus: *"Dear children, the time has come when you can no longer survive without My direct intervention. The one you call Satan is the Shining Darkness who has poisoned all your souls and has deprived you of the dignity with which I gifted each one of My children. I created each of you good. To each of you I gifted a whole and pure soul. The Shining Darkness has taken away My gift from you, your dignity.*

Satan is attacking My children of Croatia precisely because I have chosen them to be the model of My love to all My children of the world. Satan's rage will not spare My children of the Western world either while they remain convinced that they are enjoying liberty and freedom now. Never have My children delighted in sin as they do now. In Noah's time, I cleansed the world of sins that were of a lesser degree than those which My children now take delight in. In China, the Shining Darkness will appear as the victor since too few people have enough faith in Divine Intervention. I tell you that the time when you will be witnesses to My direct intervention in your earthly lives is coming soon. But I admonish you to examine your love and faithfulness to me. The Shining Darkness will multiply his powers. The Shining Darkness is preparing for a great bloodshed in the

175

Eastern world, specially in the USSR. In the Western world, My children will meet with great injustices, violent oppression, and even deeper and greater loss of dignity, the gift I gifted you with. Convert and your prayers will be answered."

[Jesus speaks to the aborted little ones]: *"Among these aborted children are a large number of those who were My gift to you for your good. The Shining Darkness knows this and he still rules your hardened hearts. These very little ones, these innocent ones were intended to deliver you from the despair which you now suffer. These innocent souls were intended to rule and advance the world which I gifted you, in the manner that I teach you, in My love. The power of faith expels the malefactor from your lives. Through your sincere love for Me you are rewarded with the power and wisdom to protect yourselves from the malefactor and all his evil. You shall destroy the empire of the Shining Darkness with conversion and prayer. The evil misuse of the press, radio, and television are now the powerful instruments of the Shining Darkness by which he blinds you and delivers the most amount of evil to you. With love that I give you, courageously put into question every institution which violates the family.*

"The Shining Darkness knows that the time of his evil reign is approaching the end. My children, be vigilant, for the Shining Darkness will multiply by his evil powers, especially where he recognizes the Divine Heavenly Presence. Everyone convert totally and you shall be the victors over the malefactor through My gifts to you. Because of your conversion, the Shining Darkness shall lose this battle, but the victims among you will be many. These are the times of My special graces for you and the Shining Darkness is deeply aware of that. By your return to My embrace, I gift you with the power to thwart all of the malefactor's intentions against which I warn you. Resist Satan tirelessly, evict him from your lives, never allow him any place among you. Out of My love for My children, I will soon wash the face of this world."

(undated)

* * * * * * * *

In this last large selection, we have many messages from both Jesus and Mary to a contemporary mystic, again from an Eastern Bloc nation, Sr. Natalia of Hungary. She was given the mission to announce Mary as *The Victorious Queen of the World*. These passages are taken from a book of the same title. Born of German stock in

Czechoslovakia, she has spent most of her adult life in Hungary as a member of the Sisters of St. Magdalene, a part of the Good Shepherd Sisters. She is still not known in the West, as her diary was only published in this country in English in 1988. Born in 1901, she still lives and continues her diary of her religious experiences. None of these entries are dated.

Jesus: *"I brought peace when I was born, but the world has not yet enjoyed it. The world is entitled to this peace. Men are children of God. God breathes His own soul into them. God cannot let Himself be put to shame and that is why the children of God are entitled to enjoy the peace that I promised."*

Sr. Natalia: "I understand that in this time of history which is so hostile to spiritual life, the souls who grow in God should stay together to make up small communities. Only in this way will life have a chance against death."

Jesus: *"If reparation and penance are done together with the Blessed Virgin Mary, they cannot be twisted so that sin could enter in. Penance done united with Her is free from imperfection. Those who unite their prayers and penances with Her do it with the faith of the Immaculate Virgin. Even if prayer and penance are done imperfectly, because of distractions, tiredness and other such things, they will be made perfect by the Immaculate Mother. We just have to ask Her sincerely and She will pray with us."*

Sr. Natalia: "Jesus showed me a Rosary of which the beads were flowers. In each flower I saw a drop of His Blood shining. When we pray the Rosary, the Blood of Jesus will fall on the person for whom we offer it. The souls of Purgatory implore the saving Blood of Jesus."

Jesus: *"The right Hand of My Father will annihilate all those sinners who will not convert despite the many warnings and the period of grace and the tireless efforts of the Church."*

Jesus: *"My daughter, tell My priests and the world that if they do not convert, then because of the multitude of sins, the world will be* *destroyed. My Words are true! Whoever listens to My Words will live; the soul was made for prayer and reverence; the heart was made for happiness and love. I am Love itself! Wherever I am loved, I live therein. Peace, silence and joy dwell in such souls. This is the reason why I remain in the tabernacles to lead souls to love and penance. If I lowered Myself to you with such a noble gesture, why then are you shy of Me?"*

Jesus: *"It is not enough to fast on bread and water. The day of fast should be also an abstinence from anger, grumbling and offending others. It should be a fasting of the lips and tongue as well."*

Sr. Natalia: *"Jesus on many occasions carried me to the place of the individual judgment of a soul. I watched as a particular soul approached the Seat of Judgment. Beside it on one side was its Guardian Angel, and on the other side Satan. Jesus awaited them in His Divine Majesty. He is the Judge and not the Father. The judgment is quick and goes on in silence. The soul could see all of its life in an instant. The soul saw all that happened not with its own eyes, but with the eyes of Jesus. It saw the black spots as bigger or smaller. If that soul will go to eternal damnation, there is no remorse in it. Jesus remains quiet, the soul turns from Him. Then Satan grabs that soul and drags it immediately to Hell. However, most of the time, Jesus with unfathomable love extends His Hand and shows the soul the place which it deserves in eternity. Then He says to it: "Go in!" Then the soul pulls a cover over itself similar to what I have seen in Purgatory and immediately goes to Purgatory. The color of the cover ranges from white to black. Our Lady goes with it, so does the Guardian Angel of the soul, both of whom try to console it. Such souls that have escaped damnation are very happy, since they have seen their place in Heaven where eternal happiness is awaiting them.*

"Our Lady is not present at all phases of the individual judgment, but before the final judgment is announced She is there and pleads with Her Son as a defense lawyer protecting Her client, particularly those who were devoted to Her life in its life. At the moment of judgment of the soul, it is completely alone in front of Jesus."

Jesus: *"Salvation does not depend on this day or yesterday, nor on a certain day forty years ago. It depends on the last moment! Therefore, you should constantly repent of your sins. You received salvation because I saved you! It is not because of your merits. Only the degree of glory that you will receive in eternity depends on your personal merits. Therefore, there are two things you constantly have* to exercise: *1) repent of your sins constantly and 2) pray often these words: 'My Jesus, I commend my soul into Your Hands.'*"

Why Hell? Sr. Natalia once asked Jesus why He created Hell. Jesus showed her the judgment of a very sinful soul whose sins He had forgiven. Satan was outraged and shouted at Jesus: "You are not just. This soul was mine all of his life. He committed so many sins and I committed only one yet you still created Hell for me." Jesus replied with love to Satan: *"Lucifer, did you ever ask forgiveness from Me?"* Lucifer went mad with rage and shouted: "Never—not that. That I will never do!" Then Jesus turned to her and said: *"You see, if he would ask forgiveness from Me only once, Hell would cease to exist."* This is why Jesus asks us to live in constant repentance of our sins. *"Every soul is a separate unique world. Not one can replace the other,"* He said. His love is very particular for each soul and is not repeated with another.

Jesus: *"Everything in Scripture must be fulfilled before the end of the world comes. Humanity is on the verge of such a bright future that will resemble Paradise where the first human couple lived. After humanity will be reborn by My cleansing grace, the happiness of Paradise will await all those who convert and live in the spirit of the Sermon on the Mount. To prepare and pray for this day to come soon, 1) live always in the holy Presence of God; 2) experience as true reality that I live in you; and 3) at every moment of your life, meet Me as I meet you."*

Jesus: *"The end of sin is near—not the end of the world! Soon the damnation of many souls will end and My words will be fulfilled and then there will be only one fold and one Shepherd."*

Sr. Natalia: "The Lord Jesus let me know that just before the victory that will bring peace to the world, great confusion and terror will reign in the Church. The cause for this confusion will be the penetration of godlessness into the closed sanctuaries of the Church; tradition will be ruined and there will be worldliness everywhere. This calamity will go together with hatred and enmity found among nations that will result in the outbreak of many wars. Many will attack the Church; their goal will be to alienate the believers from the Church and take away their trust in her. In this way they will become prey to Satan."

Sr. Natalia: "The Blessed Virgin told me that the decisive victory which will end the saturation of the world with lies and open the way of the promised holy peace will have come when Satan has gained power everywhere; when he will have seduced most souls; when he will have felt his greatest haughtiness which will know no bounds knowing that he can ruin all of God's creation including souls; when the true faith and light will live in only a few souls because all of the weak ones will have gone over to his side; then the victory will come suddenly and unexpectedly."

Sr. Natalia: "At the Second Coming, when the Heavenly Father will glorify the world, Christ will be triumphant. But before this triumph must necessarily come the victory of Mary. Her victory is the victory of grace and mercy. The victory of the sun's rays over the icy world. By the victory of the Blessed Virgin Mother, we will regain the life that was lost through Paradise's original sin. In this newly cleansed world, people will live almost without sin."

Father God: *"The world is immersed in sin and has to be destroyed according to My Justice. However, through the merciful intervention of both My Son and His Mother, mercy has prevailed. The sinful world has gained mercy on account of the supplication of the Immaculate Mother of God. We will trust the salvific work of the world to Her. To save the world She needs power. Therefore we endow the Immaculate Mother of God with the powers of Queen. Her title shall be: The Victorious Queen of the World. As Co-Redemptrix of the world, mankind, which is condemned to die because of their sins, will receive grace and salvation through Her. We place under Her command the Hosts of Angels. "*

Jesus: *"My Immaculate Mother will be victorious over sin with Her power as Queen. When My Immaculate Mother steps on the head of the serpent, the Gates of Hell will be closed forever. The Angelic Hosts will be part of this battle. I have sealed My own with My seal so that they shall not be lost in this great battle. "*

Mary: *"My child, you should know the fire ravaging in the world, the fire of Satan, is permitted by My Father. By this destructive fire, the good are being separated from evil; in this manner, the good, tried and cleansed by this fire, become noble and even better. Tell this to My children. The time for the conversion of the wicked world is hidden* *in the depths of My Immaculate Heart. Not even My Son knows this time, only the Father who locked the knowledge of it in the treasure house of My Heart. "*

Sr. Natalia: "I saw God's Holy Spirit as a devastating fire inundate the world. This fire will not bring peace nor mercy, but devastating punishment. Whenever the flame of the Holy Spirit swept through, the evil spirits by the thousands fell back into Hell. I understand that we can escape the just punishment of God only if we seek refuge under the blue mantle of our Blessed Mother and ask mercy through Her."

Sr. Natalia: "Jesus showed me that after the cleansing of mankind, people will live an angelic and clean life. There will be an end to the sins against the sixth Commandment, adultery, and an end to lies. The Savior showed me that unceasing love, happiness and divine joy will signify this future pure world. I saw the blessing of God abundantly poured out upon the earth. Satan and sin were completely defeated and took leave."

Jesus: *"The power of My Immaculate Mother, your Queen will overcome all enemies! The Eternal Father has given Her this power as a gift. The victory will be Hers even if Hell and the world attack Her with all their united power! The victory of My Immaculate Mother will be realized as it was decided on at the moment of creation by the Holy Trinity. I endowed My Mother with My divine power and all members of the Holy Trinity blessed Her. "*

1986

Sr. Natalia: *"The Lord let me see a beautiful reddish globe the size of an infant's head seen at a great distance. It traveled on a transparent cloud. It arrived from the East and stopped for a few seconds over Hungary, Her country. The sphere then opened and from it our Mother came out as the Queen of the World. She moved over the cloud to glance down over Hungary, Her own possession, and showered Her Hungarian children with graces. Everybody could see Her, and this itself was one of the graces. The hearts of the people suddenly burned with love toward God and their fellow man. Penitence poured out from them and their souls seemingly became* *freed from the burden of their sins. At that same moment, everybody fell in the dust of their sins while their hands and eyes turned upwards toward Heaven crying out for mercy. There were only a few people who didn't ask for this mercy, and of these, many died. This vision is the forerunner of the great miracle promised to the world. The Heavenly Mother then flew over us traveling further to the place where the promised grace of the great miracle will happen. "*

January 24, 1986

Mary: *"Be not afraid! The peace which is the gift of My Son for those who believe in Him will not take long in coming. It will come through Me and it is very near you. This peace which My Son brought at His birth—and the world has not yet enjoyed—will be here before the next century. Trust in Me! I solemnly tell you, this generation shall not pass away until these things happen. "*

1985

Consecrations and Prayers

We have been lovingly asked by Our Lady to pray with our hearts. We have been asked to consecrate our hearts to the Hearts of Jesus and Mary. I have included consecrations, the Miracle Prayer, and the Prayer to St. Michael; and I have added the prayer given by Our Lady at Conyers to be echoed throughout the world.

Consecration to Jesus Christ
Through the Blessed Virgin Mary
According to St. Louis De Montfort

O Eternal and Incarnate Wisdom! O sweetest and most adorable Jesus! True God and true man, only Son of the Eternal Father, and of Mary, always virgin! I adore Thee profoundly in the bosom and splendors of the virginal bosom of Mary, Thy most worthy Mother, in the time of Thine Incarnation.

I give Thee thanks for that Thou hast annihilated Thyself, taking the form of a slave in order to rescue me from the cruel slavery of the devil. I praise and glorify Thee for that Thou hast been pleased to submit Thyself to Mary, Thy Holy Mother, in all things, in order to make me Thy Faithful slave through Her. But, alas! Ungrateful and faithless as I have been, I have not kept the promises which I made so solemnly to Thee in Baptism; I have not fulfilled my obligations; I do not deserve to be called Thy child, not yet Thy slave; and as there is nothing in me which does not merit Thine anger and Thy repulse, I dare not come by myself before Thy most holy and august Majesty. It is on this account that I have recourse to the intercession of Thy most Holy Mother, whom Thou hast given me for a mediatrix with Thee. It is through Her that I hope to obtain of Thee contrition, the pardon of my sins, and the acquisition and preservation of wisdom.

Hail, then, O Immaculate Mary, living tabernacle of the Divinity, where the Eternal Wisdom willed to be hidden and to be adored by angels and by men! Hail, O Queen of Heaven and earth, to whose empire everything is subject which is under God. Hail, O sure refuge of sinners, whose mercy fails no one. Hear the desire which I have of the Divine Wisdom; and for that end receive the vows and offerings which in my lowliness I present.

> I, _____, a faithless sinner, renew and ratify today in Thy hands the vows of my Baptism;
> I renounce forever Satan, his pomps and works; and I give myself
> entirely to Jesus Christ, the Incarnate Wisdom, to
> carry my cross after Him all the days of my life, and to be more
> faithful to Him than I have ever been before.
> In the presence of all the heavenly court, I choose Thee this day
> for my Mother and Mistress. I deliver and consecrate to Thee,
> as Thy slave, my body and soul, my goods, both interior and exterior,
> and even the value of all my good actions, past, present and future; leaving to Thee the entire and full right of disposing of me,
> and all that belongs to me, without exception, according to
> Thy good pleasure, for the greater glory of God, in time and in eternity.

Receive, O benignant Virgin, this little offering of my slavery, in honor of, and in union with, that subjection which the Eternal Wisdom deigned to have to Thy maternity, both in homage to the power which You have over this poor sinner, and in thanksgiving for the privileges with which the Holy Trinity has favored Thee. I declare that I wish henceforth, as Thy true slave, to seek Thy honor and to obey Thee in all things.

O admirable Mother, present me to Thy dear Son as His eternal slave, so that as He has redeemed me by Thee, by Thee He may receive me! O Mother of mercy, grant me the grace to obtain the true Wisdom of God; and for that end receive me among those whom Thou lovest and teachest, who Thou leadest, nourishest and protectest as Thy children and Thy slaves.

O faithful Virgin, make me in all things so perfect a disciple, imitator and slave of the Incarnate Wisdom, Jesus Christ Thy Son, that I may attain, by Thine intercession and by Thine example, to the fullness of His age on earth and of His glory in Heaven. Amen.

Signed: _____

Date: _____

CONSECRATION TO THE HEART OF JESUS

O Jesus, we know that You are sweet*
That You have given Your Heart for us.
It was crowned with thorns by our sins.
We know that today You still pray for us
so that we will not be lost.
Jesus, remember us if we fall into sin.
Through Your most Sacred Heart,
make us all love one another.
Cause hatred to disappear among men.
Show us Your love.
All of us love You.
And we desire that You protect us with Your
Heart of the Good Shepherd.
Enter into each heart, Jesus!
Knock on the door of our hearts.
Be patient and tenacious with us.
We are still locked up in ourselves, because we
have not understood Your will.
Knock continuously, Oh Jesus.
Make our hearts open up to You,
at least when we remember the passion
which You suffered for us. Amen.

*Mt. 11:20

CONSECRATION TO THE IMMACULATE
HEART OF MARY

O Immaculate Heart of Mary, overflowing
with goodness, Show us Your love for us.
May the flame of Your heart, Oh Mary,
Descend upon all peoples.
We love You immensely.
Impress in our hearts a true love.
May our hearts yearn for You.
Oh Mary, sweet and humble of heart,
Remember us when we sin.
You know that we men are sinners.
Through Your most sacred and maternal
heart,
Cure us from every spiritual illness.
Make us capable of looking at the beauty
of Your maternal heart,
And that, thus, we may be converted
to the flame of Your heart. Amen.

PRAYER TO ST. MICHAEL
Composed by Pope Leo XIII (1878-1903)
and formerly said after low Mass in Catholic Churches.

Saint Michael, the Archangel, defend us in battle, be our defense against the wickedness and snares of the devil. May God rebuke him, we humbly pray; and do thou, O Prince of the heavenly host, by the power of God, thrust into Hell Satan and the other evil spirits who prowl about the world for the ruin of souls. Amen.

THE MIRACLE PRAYER

Lord Jesus, I come before You, just as I am. I am sorry for my sins, I repent of my sins, please forgive me. In Your name, I forgive all others for what they have done against me. I renounce satan, the evil spirits and all their works. I give You my entire self. Lord Jesus, now and forever, I invite You into my life. Jesus, I accept You as my Lord, God and Savior. Heal me, change me, strengthen me in body, soul and spirit.

Come Lord Jesus, cover me with Your precious blood and fill me with Your Holy Spirit, I Love You Lord Jesus. I Praise You Jesus. I Thank You Jesus. I shall follow You every day of my life. Amen.

[Say this Prayer faithfully, no matter how you feel; when you come to the point where you sincerely mean each word, with all your heart, something good spiritually will happen to you. You will experience Jesus, and He will change your whole life in a very special way. You will see.]

Most Holy Trinity—
Father, Son, and Holy
Spirit—I adore Thee
profoundly. I offer Thee
the most precious Body,
Blood, Soul and Divinity
of Jesus Christ, present in
all the tabernacles of the
world, in reparation for
the outrages, sacrileges and
indifferences whereby He
is offended. And through
the infinite merits of His
Most Sacred Heart and
the Immaculate Heart
of Mary, I beg of
Thee the conversion
of poor sinners.

"Let this prayer be echoed
all over the world."

Our Loving Mother's Children
Post Office Box 309
Conyers, Georgia 30207
U.S.A.

Questions and Answers

Frequently I am asked many questions about Nancy. I will try to answer a few based on lectures already given. Some questions are asked again and again.

Is there a way that Nancy knows for sure that the Lord speaks to her?

Certainly faith is a factor here, but Jesus and Mary, in Their love, also want Nancy to be reassured. They ask her to test the visions she receives by casting them out in the name of Jesus. The Lord has asked her to sprinkle holy water at the visions. Nancy also asks them to say "I bow down to God the Father and worship Him with my whole heart, mind and being." Naturally, Satan would have difficulty with this.

I believe that "we will know them by their fruits." The fruits of Conyers appear positive, loving and plentiful. There are many signs, wonders and healings, and people are converting their hearts.

Which is more significant—physical healing or spiritual healing?

We forget we are on a journey back to God. We forget why we are here. Which would be more helpful in your journey back to God? When you answer this you will have answered your question.

Why is the Blessed Mother appearing?

I suppose we need only to pick up a paper, turn on a TV or look around our own environment to answer this. Look at broken relationships, murder, rape, suicide, depression and tragedy. We have become computerized and depersonalized. How appropriate that Christ would send His Mother. She represents love, compassion, gentleness and nurturing. Are these not the qualities missing in today's society?

Why do you think she is appearing to Nancy?

Why not? Nancy is every person. She is a wife and mother. She represents many of us. God is not calling us to extraordinary lives, but simple lives extraordinarily led. God is no chooser of persons. He loves us all. What better way to demonstrate this? Nancy said she was not deserving to see Christ. Who is deserving? We all have our imperfections, but God loves us right where we are with all our frailties.

What if Mary is not there?
If we experience a conversion of heart. . .if we return our lives to God. . .does it matter? It is my conviction, however, that She is there, but also with us here now. The greatest wonder is seeing people from all over and all faiths come together in love in this name.

We keep hearing pray from the heart. How?

God knows us. He wants an intimate relationship with Him. Nancy is proof of that. He already knows our innermost thoughts. The expectation is that we will pray with honesty and sincerity and not just an insincere "polly parrot" of words. Nancy has said God is our best friend. We should approach Him accordingly.

Why are there so many visions taking place?

God is trying to get our attention. Look around. Every 78 seconds a child commits suicide. Look at Baghdad and Somalia. Consider the current suffering in Yugoslavia. Look at the abortion figures. How about child abuse? Depressions? Psychiatrists' offices are filled. Churches are not. We need to return our lives to the Healer of Healers. We need to come back to God. These visions represent an urgency. There will be consequences for our actions.

You said that Jesus spoke to Nancy about "being little". . .What does that mean?
We are talking about humility often misunderstood. There must be a submission to the will of God, a respect for God's will versus our own. We do not perform great acts of love, but rather God is working through us. This awareness is "being little." Our egos are diminished and inner humility emerges.

What about people who focus on their miraculous photos or the phenomena in the sky?

We need only be concerned if we are one of these people. Each is on his own journey. Each one of us is called to live the love. Remember, phenomena can only hold our attention for a short while. Our Lady said to pray every day for the grace of greater faith.

Should people go to Conyers?

This is a question that can only be answered at an individual level. The ideal is to find Christ in our hearts in this moment and right here and right now. For some, this is difficult. Certainly the signs and wonders are available in Conyers.

What is the greatest sin? Does Jesus talk about this to Nancy?

One of the most grievous offenses is to despair of Jesus' love and mercy. Nancy has said, "If only Judas had said I am sorry, Lord." Christ's love and mercy are infinite.

What is the difference between prayer and meditations?

If you look for definitions, prayer is talking to God and meditation is listening to God.

Should a person pray for healing?

One should pray that God's will be done. God in His wisdom knows what is best for each soul. We must trust His Infinite Wisdom.

Does Jesus talk about rationalization at Conyers?

Yes! On June 1, 1991, Jesus said, *"Man no longer calls sin sin. Man no longer knows Me. Man no longer seeks Me and deserves Me.*

Is Christ really upset with us?

This is what he said on December 31, 1990:
"The time has come for My justice. I call and I call and I call and My children do not respond. They do not come. . . Murder is in their hearts. They murder the unborn. They murder the born. They murder the old. They murder the young. They murder the well. They murder the disabled. They slander My name, mock Me. "

What if the apparitions are not approved by your church?

The church (Catholic) does not require that we believe in and accept apparitions. There are many who require a sign to rekindle their faith. God in His Love has provided them in over 300 locations in the world. Many are under investigation by the church.

I would add the following attributed to Pope Urban VIII: "In cases which concern private revelations, it is better to believe than not to believe, for if you believe, and it is proven true, you will be happy that you have believed, because our Holy Mother asked it. If you believe, and it should be proven false, you will receive all the blessings as if it had been true, because you believed it to be so."

Remember, Jesus is interested in our hearts.

Why do some people have so much trouble believing in supernatural events?

I cannot speak for everyone, but I firmly believe that the mind has great difficulty when the heart strays from the home. I try to lead with my heart and yet maintain a balance.

I am Jewish; what do you say to me?

There is only One! He will not have strange Gods before Him. We all honor the "One." We all need to remember we are on a journey back to Him and live our lives accordingly in love.

I don't understand your Catholic Confession. Can you help?

I hope so. As Catholics, we perceive the priest as the representative of Christ on earth, so there is no difficulty sharing the pain and weaknesses that trouble us. There is total confidentiality. It is like speaking to a loving Father who provides help and reassurance in our spiritual journeys.

As a non-Catholic it is important that one be sorry for offending God. It is important to make retribution and to amend one's life. God knows our hearts. Atonement must take place within one's own heart and with God.

What about the earthquakes and natural disasters?

We need to focus on the Lord. If we keep our eyes on Him, He will take care of the fear. Love replaces fear. He has promised not to leave us.

Appendix 1: Correspondence From the Office of the Archbishop of Atlanta Concerning the Apparitions at Conyers

[The Archbishop's letters are reprinted from *Mother of Great Love, Mother of Great Sorrow*, by Ron Tesoriero (Central Coast Target Marketing, 1992).]

MEMORANDUM

FROM: Archbishop Lyke
TO: The Priests of the Archdiocese of Atlanta
SUBJECT: The Alleged Apparitions at Conyers
DATE: January 17, 1992

It has come to my attention that priests who minister in the Archdiocese of Atlanta have been asked to lead pilgrimages to see the alleged apparitions in Conyers. May I state the following as policy:

Priests are not to accept invitations to lead pilgrimages or visits to Conyers, nor are they to initiate such. Further, parishes are not to sponsor pilgrimages or visits, nor are meetings and prayer groups directly related to these alleged apparitions to take place in our parishes.

Moreover, I have not given nor do I intend to give permission for the celebration of the Eucharist on the grounds where the alleged apparitions take place. I ask that all priests of the Archdiocese, as well as any other priest who may visit the site of the alleged apparitions, respect my wishes in this regard.

(I have made arrangements with Father John Walsh to provide suitable pastoral care at St. Pius X. Further, the monks of the Trappist Monastery permit the pilgrims to come to the monastery church and grounds.)

Please understand. It is important that we not create the

perception or impression that I or the Archdiocese endorse or authenticate these alleged apparitions.

Lastly, I refer you again to my statement of September 10, 1991 on this matter.

Thank you very much for your consideration.

Archdiocese of Atlanta
    680 West Peachtree Street N.W., Atlanta Georgia 30308-1984 (404) 888-7804 Fax (404) 885-7494

* * * * * *

September 10, 1991

The Catholic Church recognizes the phenomenon known as visions, or more popularly, apparitions. In the past, the Church has declared certain of these events as "worthy of pious belief," notably : Guadalupe (1531), to Catherine Laboure (1830), LaSalette (1846), Lourdes (1858), and Fatima (1917).

Visions are defined as charisms freely bestowed by God, for the spiritual benefit of the Faithful.

The Fathers of the Second Vatican Council reminded us in Lumen Gentium (#66-67) that a balanced attitude must be maintained towards the place of special cults in our devotional life. As such, we must not allow them to distract us from the central mysteries and liturgical rites that constitute the principal means of expression for the worshipping Faithful. Such a distraction from the essential faith would seriously compromise possible authenticity, as would any self-gain on the part of the visionary (-ies) or their associates.

On the other hand, we cannot deny the possibility that God might continue to disclose Himself by means of timely or historical self-revelation. If the Faithful are truly elevated and brought closer to the central "vision" of the Gospel, the appearance of Jesus Christ in history as God and man, by a vision or series of apparitions, then the Church must lend herself to a serious investigation into their possible authenticity.

Recently, claims have been made that Christ, as well as

the Blessed Virgin Mary have appeared in Rockdale County. At this time, circumstances do not warrant a formal investigation into these events; however, Archbishop Lyke is aware of these reports, and will monitor closely the reaction of the local Church with regard to this matter. We should recall that the Church has always approached events of this nature with great caution, and advisedly so. Scripture cautions us:

Leave them alone, for if this plan and work of theirs is a man-made thing, it will disappear; but if it comes from God you cannot possibly defeat them. (Acts 5:38-39)

In the meantime, those Catholics who feel drawn by these events are urged to remember that the sacramental life of the parish must remain the central activity for the worshipping Faithful. It is the Eucharist which nourishes our faith, and to which our first devotion is due. As these matters undergo examination, and in the absence of any authoritative opinion, Archbishop Lyke has stated that no parish facilities may be used for the fostering of any devotion to matters lacking Church approval. However, pastors and their assistants are asked to be ready to offer counselling and reassurance to any who approach them with questions regarding these events.

Because of the proximity of the Cistercian Community at the Monastery of Our Lady of the Holy Spirit, many of the Faithful have been attracted to this holy place, gathering for prayer and discussion. This is understandable in the light of the Church's tradition, for monastic communities are rightly considered to be well-springs of spiritual power. However, the Faithful are urged to consider the special contemplative nature of this community, living, as they do, in a close family relationship, and generally harbored by the holy rule of cloistered life. No eternal event, no matter how seemingly significant, must be allowed to impinge on this special part of the family of the Church of North Georgia. The normal daily prayer-life of the monks is an inestimable aid to the faith of the local Church, and any disruption of that life can only compromise a timely and reasonable consideration of the purported apparitions.

Accordingly, Archbishop Lyke has asked Abbot Bernard and the Monks to cease any direct relationship with the activities and events surrounding the purported apparitions in Rockdale County. While the Faithful may participate in the monastic liturgies and devotions, as permitted, the monks themselves may not engage in counselling, discussion-groups or visits related to the purported apparitions.

* * * * * *

March 6, 1992

To all Bishops of the United States

My dear brother Bishop:

I write to ask your assistance in a matter that has become a significant issue for the welfare of the Church in this area.

For some time now, there have been claims that the Blessed Mother is appearing to a lady who lives in Conyers, Georgia—a town about 45 miles outside of Atlanta. Various groups, principally from the southeast, have begun to organize "pilgrimages" to the site—especially around the 13th of each month, which is when the apparitions are alleged principally to occur, and that these pilgrimages are being promoted from the pulpit in many cases.

I have issued a directive to the priests who minister in the Archdiocese of Atlanta (a copy is enclosed). It has now come to my attention that numerous priests (many leading pilgrimages) are coming to Conyers, and that Mass is being offered at the site contrary to my expressed directive. These activities, and the presence of priests and religious in large numbers, are being used as evidence of authenticity, as is the existence of a chapel which was established without my authorization.

It is my considered judgment that the authenticity of these alleged apparitions is in grave doubt. Certainly, the welfare of the local Church dictates that I take some further action at least to discourage these pilgrimages and to regulate liturgical practices within my jurisdiction.

Accordingly, I ask your assistance in two ways:

(i) Would you please convey to your priests (or others as you think appropriate) my wishes that pilgrimages to Conyers not be organized. It is especially problematic when these are promoted from the pulpit.

(ii) Would you please do what you can to convey to your priests my express directive that no Eucharistic celebration is to take place at the site of the alleged apparitions. I want the priests who visit the area to understand clearly that this is not a request but an explicit directive in accordance with the provisions of canon 838, #3, C.I.C.

I deeply appreciate any assistance you can give me in getting this situation under control.

In the Peace of Christ,

Most Reverend James P. Lyke, O.F.M., Ph.D.
Archbishop of Atlanta

enclosure: copy of memo from January 17, 1992

Archdiocese of Atlanta
680 West Peachtree Street, N.W. Atlanta, Georgia 30308-1984 (404) 888-7804 Fax (404) 885-7492

Appendix 2: The Holy Hill at Conyers

The Holy Hill at Conyers

Jesus has declared *the little insignificant, very ordinary hill* in Nancy's backyard to be Holy and calls on His children to visit Him there. Jesus has said to the visionary Nancy, *"I, Jesus, am calling all My children here...Come in numbers and show Me your faith."* Jesus is appearing every day to Nancy. *"Where are My Children?"* Jesus has also blessed the well water and promises to heal His *children who come in faith.*

All are invited to visit and pray any day on His Holy Hill at the altar in the shape of a cross. Jesus said to Nancy, *"I solemnly tell you, who comes to the altar with faith, I will pour forth My graces. Oh, what gifts they will walk away with."* The Blessed Mother said, *"When the father comes with gifts for his family, everyone is happy and anxious to open the presents and they open the gifts and see that they are all very fine gifts but then, they leave the gifts behind and walk away from the father. My dear children, the gifts from the Father are fine and priceless here at Conyers. It is up to you to receive them or to not come."* [She is crying.]

Many conversions, healings and signs are taking place. Jesus has said, *"Gold dust will fall from Heaven. Rosaries will turn golden color and hearts will be converted. I am healing My children. Go and believe."* This and much more has been witnessed including the miracle of the sun. Pilgrims are welcome during the week from 9 AM to 7 PM to come visit the farm. Also, at Nancy's pilgrims may pray on the Holy Hill, obtain the Blessed well water and make the Stations of the Cross.

Directions to the Holy Hill

From Atlanta, Ga. area take I-285 to Exit #35. This puts you on

I-20 East toward Augusta, Ga. Take I-20 East to Exit #42 (one of the Conyers exits) and turn left (north) onto Highway #138 North. Go exactly 4.9 miles north on Hwy. 138. Turn left onto White Road. The Farm is 0.3 miles on the left at 2324 White Road, Conyers, Ga 30207 (phone 404/922-8885).

Information concerning the events at Conyers, books available and the current message and Journal are available free. To receive this information, send a stamped, self-addressed business size envelope. Send envelopes to:

Our Loving Mother's Children
Post Office Box 675, Newington, Virginia 22122

Current Message—703/503-7991   Information—404/922-8885

Please Help Us Begin Documentation of
the Conyers Apparitions

We have begun a process to document the Video and Still Image sightings that are witnessed here. WE NEED YOUR HELP. We are compiling this information in a computer program in hopes that one day the Church will want the documentation.

1. When you take the pictures please try to make a note or mental note as to your location on the grounds.

2. When you have your film developed have the pictures developed at a reliable, national developing company, so that when the church does begin investigating this miracle we will be able to say that no one to our knowledge has modified or superimposed the images that are on the picture. Most film today is developed automatically and this does not allow for human intervention.

3. When you have the pictures developed, take advantage of the 2-for-1 offers. We do not want to take away your only picture.

4. Keep the negatives. Negatives can be analyzed to determine the pictures' validity. We are not questioning your honesty but others might.

5. On the back of the picture write the following:

1. Your name (First, Last);
2. Your telephone number;
3. Your address;
4. A brief description of what is in the picture;
5. What date the picture was taken; and
6. Sign the photo and date it.

Then mail it to:

Our Loving Mother's Children
Attn: Documentation
Post Office Box 309
Conyers, Ga 30208

Other books about the apparitions at Conyers, Georgia:

Conversion Journey to Light, by Kevin Boyer (Newington, VA: Our Loving Mother's Children, 1992).

Mother of Great Love, Mother of Great Sorrow, by Ron Tesoriero (Central Coast Target Marketing, 1992). [A video tape of Ron Tesorios's material is also available from Our Loving Mother's Children, P.O. Box 675, Newington, VA 22122.]

To Bear Witness that I Am the Living Son of God, Volumes I and II, by Nancy Fowler (Newington, VA: Our Loving Mother's Children, 1992).

Ann Marie Hancock has recorded on video tape a series of interviews concerning the apparitions at Medjugorje:

1. *Our Lady's Message of Conversion,* with Fr. Phillip Pavich, Archbishop Fran Franic, and visionaries Jakov Colo, Ivan Dragicevic, and Vicka.

2. *Our Lady's Message of Love,* with Fr. Svetozar Kraljevic.

3. *Our Lady's Message of Healing,* with pilgrims who've experienced healings in Medjugorje.

4. *Our Lady's Message of Fasting,* with Slavko Barbaric.

5. *Our Lady's Message of Consecrating Our Hearts to Mary,* with Fr. Phillip Pavich.

6. *Our Lady's Message of Prayer,* with Fr. Jozo Zovko.

These video tapes are available through:

A-Plus Keepsake Video, Inc.
177 Ballantine Road
Middletown, NJ 07748
ph. 908-957-0005

Author's Note:
More Reflections

On May 13, 1993, I returned to Conyers to capture the cover photo for this book. Tens of thousands of people were present from all over the world. The first man to whom I was introduced was a priest from Peru. Later, standing on the porch, I met a priest who came from Puerto Rico to see Nancy.

Most interesting was the number of purported visionaries from different parts of the world, including Canada and Venezuela:

Veronique DeMers is fifteen years old and is from Ontario, Canada. She drove with her family of four for two days to arrive in time for the apparition on May 13. When I asked Veronique why she came, she said, "The Blessed Mother asked me to come here today."

Chrys Moore is a purported visionary from Oklahoma. So is Shawna Flenniken. Both received messages from The Blessed Mother to come to Conyers.

José Luis Matthews of Maracaibo, Venezuela, is a purported visionary. At The Blessed Mother's suggestion through José, Nancy Fowler was invited to Maracarbo on March 25, 1993. After Easter 1993, José received a message to go to Conyers in May. Another visionary from Venezuela, Juan Antonio GilGil was also told to go to Conyers by The Holy Mother.

These events alone are mind-boggling. There is more, however; Nancy also had mystical experiences while in Venezuela simultaneously with José and Juan. Much of this information is private and cannot be shared yet.

I asked Juan if The Blessed Mother is joining key visionaries and others together for a purpose. He smiled when the interpreter, Tania Garcia, uttered the words to him. He grinned widely and said, "There will be a gathering, but I can share no more."

It was fascinating to meet all of these people from various countries, but even more interesting was what The Blessed Mother had prepared for the gathering which included these visitors. Present also were representatives from "Inside Edition," CBS Chicago, independent New York film makers, Miami and South Carolina television stations, and all Atlanta television stations. The Blessed Mother orchestrated a show unlike any I have ever seen.

When Nancy announced that The Blessed Mother was departing, a funnel cloud formed in the sky; it was filmed by national television. Rose petals dropped from the sky; many were witness to this. Hail fell from the sky and some said it fell in square shapes. The trees bent in half, followed by torrential rain. Later, the sky was as blue as a robin's egg, and the sun came out. God was totally in control!

Ann Marie Hancock (left), son Chip, husband Tom, daughters (standing from left) Faith and Cori

About The Author:

Ann Marie Hancock is also the author of *Be a Light: Miracles at Medjugorje*.

Ms. Hancock has been happily married for more than twenty years to Thomas F. Hancock and has three children, Cori, Faith, and Chip. She is a former TV personality, model, and talk show host. Her accomplishments include:

* Award—American Academy of Pediatrics on behalf of the International Year of the Child
* Past member, National Presswomen
* Member, International Platform Association for Select Speakers in the United States and Abroad
* Top Television Personality in Virginia 1980
* Red Cross "Breath of Life" Award for Devotion to Humanity
* First Media Recipient—Virginia Rehabilitation Association Award

She will complete her Master's Degree in Humanities at the University of Richmond in the fall of 1993.

She currently lives in Midlothian, Virginia, with her husband and children.

Ann Marie Hancock is available for lectures on the apparitions of Mary. For information, please write:

Ann Marie Hancock
P.O. Box 243
Midlothian, VA 23113

Hampton Roads publishes a variety of books on metaphysical,
spiritual, health-related, and general interest subjects.
Would you like to be notified as we publish new books in your area of
interest? If you would like a copy of our latest catalog, just call
toll-free, (800) 766-8009, or send your name and address to:

Hampton Roads Publishing Company, Inc.
891 Norfolk Square
Norfolk, VA 23502